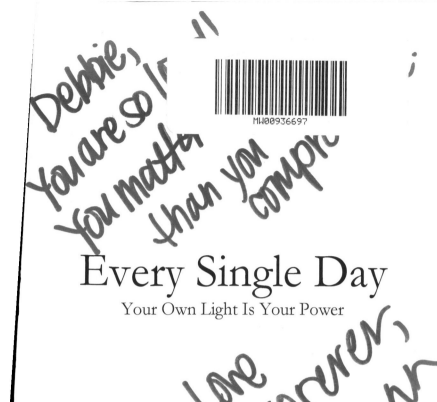

Debbie,
You are so l[...]
You matt[...]
than you compr[...]

Every Single Day
Your Own Light Is Your Power

Love
Forever,
Laurann

Laurann Turner

DEDICATION

I dedicate this book to you. To all of you. I dedicate it to those of you who have felt heartache, sadness, confusion, anger, or despair. For those of you whose dreams haven't come true. For any of you who are struggling with a situation wondering why it is happening to you. To any of you who feel lost, helpless or incomplete. To any of you who are unsatisfied with your life. I also dedicate this book to those of you who are happy and living the life of your dreams. May this book remind you of your fortune.

Thank you for being here and for reading my book.

CONTENTS

ACKNOWLEDGMENTS

For the last seven or so years I have been telling people I wanted to write a book. The story line of the book changed a few times but the message always came back to the same idea. I wanted to write a book about being confident. No that I am an expert on this subject. I was born wanting to pave my own path in life. I've always had a strong desire to learn and understand as many things as possible. Through life experiences I found myself in a situation that left me examining things. I was living a very good life but deep inside of me I knew something was missing. I lost my zeal. My excitement. My confidence had dimmed. I struggled to know my life's purpose.

It took me years once I became an adult to understand how to have a grown up relationship with my parents. I figured it out when I realized they were people who had struggles in their lives just like I have struggles. They needed to have someone to lean on and to listen to them just as I needed those things. They have become some of my dearest and greatest friends. They keep me grounded. They are my absolute best supporters. I do not have a single doubt that they would give their very lives for me if necessary. Understanding this gives me a great foundation for who I am.

My siblings are no different, they, with their spouses and kids give me support daily. They are among my most enthusiastic fans. They have watched me as the youngest sibling, grow, stumble, pick myself up and keep going. They effortlessly continue to show me love, support and encouragement.

I went through a great process of change that started in the spring of 2016. I changed the entire landscape of my life including my job, my home, relationships, my hair, my understanding of what has worth, and my perception of what is important. I learned that there was a light and power inside of me that allows me to live a very bold, unapologetically happy life. I work daily to be my very best, most authentic self. Although I strive for this, I still struggle with common doubts and fears of what I am able to accomplish. The one thing I constantly remind myself is that one day I will die and all of the things I worry about or want to control won't matter. With that said, here is my story, the story of finding my own light which has become my most incredible source of power.

This book is my journey. My journey from a place of not being happy to a place of joy and security. These are my thoughts, experiences and emotions. Others may have experienced these things differently. I love that part of the human experience. That we can all be ourselves. There is no one else like us. May all of us find joy, peace, truth and happiness on our journey. May all of our hopes and dreams come true.

Laurann Turner

THE BOX

I looked up into his cloudy blue eyes. He was a bit taller
than me. He had dark brown hair that had grown out over
his ears a little. His short beard and mustache were a dark
auburn color. How had I gotten so lucky? I had waited so
long for this moment. He loved me and I knew it. I had
finally met the man of my dreams. His lips were the
perfect shade of natural pink. When he hugged me I felt
safe, I felt connected, I was adored and cherished.

Our hearts raced every time we were close. Although
we had only been a couple for a few months, each time he
kissed me it felt like our first. He was magical. He was
undeniably everything I had always been looking for. He
was smart, talented, witty, strong, kind and giving. At times
my heart and mind couldn't believe this was real.

He bent down to kiss me goodnight. I grinned, my
heart fluttered, and then I heard …. sniff, sniff, (the sound
of a whimper). What? What was that? Where am I? I

1

slowly opened my eyes. What just happened? I was just about to get kissed by the man of my dreams.

Looking over to the side of my bed. There he was, Charlie, my eight-year-old boxer. It was morning and time for him to have a potty break. "Hi Char Char. Do you need to go potty?" He grunted and let out another familiar whine. "Okay, let's go." I had been dreaming. I thought to myself, "that was an intense dream" as I got out of my perfectly comfortable king-sized bed. I've never had such a vivid dream like that before. I wonder what it meant? I wish it were real. I wish a man like that existed. I let out a sigh filled with a touch of sadness and a bit of despair. There was nothing in my life like that gorgeous, handsome man who was just about to kiss me. It had been a dream. A very good dream but a dream nonetheless.

I opened the door of my quaintly decorated bedroom that had been professionally painted in a two-toned color scheme I had found on Pinterest. The painter I used was the adult son of a neighbor. He was so detailed and fast I used him to paint all of the bedrooms in my house and hallway. "Come on Char let's go outside."

We stepped out into the hallway; our feet touch the refinished original hard wood cherry oak floors. We walked past the guest bedroom where the bed sat perfectly undisturbed and always made. We passed my home office. Walking down the hall I glanced at my framed Master's and Bachelor's degrees. I worked hard to get those pieces of paper I think I should have them displayed.

Charlie choose to go through the living room and around the kitchen table to the double French doors that led out to the deck. I walked through my newly remodeled kitchen. Another carefully executed Pinterest copy with dark gray walls, white quartz counter tops, white subway tile back splash and white custom-built cabinets.

some ❤ HEARTS understand Each Other even in SILENCE [1]

"Here you go Char." I opened the back door. Charlie trotted outside to his favorite spot and squatted to take care of his morning business.

I left the door cracked open for Charlie to come back in when finished. I went to my stainless-steel fridge and took out spinach, avocado, blueberries, and cucumbers to make a smoothie. I thought about my dream. My heart felt sad. I wish the dream had been real. It wasn't real. I'm 36 years old and alone. Single. Never married. With no one in sight to marry. I looked out my kitchen window. I saw the

---

[1] To access printable artwork visit www.everysingledaycorporation.com

hot tub on my deck, the cherry tree in the backyard with its beautiful blossoms. The grape vines on my brown and white shed were starting to show green leaves. I had made a beautiful life for myself. A lovely home that was a great representation of me. I worked hard to gain a great education. So, why didn't I feel happier?

Charlie came running back inside. He is always happiest in the morning. He jaunted down the hallway and stopped for a drink. I followed him so I could give him his medicine. He had to have it twice a day. His thyroid stopped working years ago after I adopted him. He was everything to me. I rescued him from the dog shelter but as people say, he also rescued me.

As I went into the room to give Charlie his medicine I saw the box. The white and blue storage box that was sitting on my office floor. The box I brought home with me the day before. The box that contained what remained of my nine-year career as a Director and Vice President of Operations for a health care company.

A surge of memories came flooding forward as I glance over the contents. I had really loved my job. I gave my life to my career. Helping the owners to build it from the beginning. That job became my heart and soul. And now, I was looking at what was left of it in a storage box. There was an orange ceramic-framed photo of me with my sister and her family in Antigua. A poster I had in my office of my favorite Colombian soccer player, a picture of Charlie, a few pictures of friends from a charity event we had gone to a few years earlier, an old radio, a silver mesh pencil holder and desk organizer. There were a few pens, pencils and post-it-notes. That was it. The representation of the last decade of my life was sitting there on the floor in a banker's storage box.

I sat down next to Charlie and without hesitation the tears began to fall. How had this happened? How had I gotten to a place where I had worked so hard for so long and now all I had to show for it was a box? It was as if my life was worth no more than the contents of that box. How had my life come to this? I was lonely and very sad.

MOVING ON

Buzz. Buzz. A text was coming through from my new co-worker. "Hey! Happy Monday! Are you still good to meet today at 11:30?" Before I quit my job, I accepted a position with a new startup company. This wasn't the first time I was going to work for a start-up. In fact, I loved working with new companies from the ground up. It was intriguing for me to be a part of a company's beginning stages. The difference this time was this was a finance company. I was taking a chance in an entirely different industry and on a new position.

I needed a major change in my life and I wanted to get away from the situation I had at my previous job. "That works for me. See you in a little bit." We were meeting to review the next step in my training process. I was excited for the new opportunity.

When we met up my new co-worker asked how I was doing. She knew leaving my previous employer had been a difficult decision. It was a small, efficiently run company that had numerous hospital accounts and many independent contractors. I was the first person the owners had hired to be a part of the company. I remember being very honored when the opportunity came to me. They were very persistent about having me be on their team. I was impressed with their kind hearts and innovative natures. The owners were creative and I loved being a part of it. They listened to my suggestions and we worked very well together. Somewhere along the way things changed. I went from being employed by people who valued others and their abilities, to being employed by people who barely gave input about the company and its standing. The owners had also moved to a different part of the country from where the headquarters of the business were located. Working there became a chore instead of that created joy in my life.

The last year I was employed there was the most difficult. During that year, three different government agencies came to the business headquarters. The government agencies were the Food and Drug Administration, the IRS and the FBI. The FBI brought with them members of the Department of Justice, and Health and Human Services. A side from the government agencies coming to the office for audits, Worker's Compensation Fund came and the insurance company who provided our product liability insurance. It felt like a steady stream of inquiry. Luckily the company was well organized and no issues were presented with any of the audits. The difficult part was that neither of the owners made themselves available to help or be involved during any of the audits. The responsibility of the audits rested on my shoulders. It was exhausting. I was tired and felt used and undervalued. I ran on very little sleep and had little time to do things I wanted.

I hadn't received a wage increase in three years and my bonuses were a third of what they had been. I was lucky to be working but these things were hard to accept. Other employees had received annual increases in their salaries. The fact that I hadn't became aggravating. I couldn't convince the owners that there were some things happening that needed their attention. They were no longer innovating; they were no longer on the forefront of the industry. They lost their passion for designing state of the art health care devices and tools. Other unforeseen company and personal difficulties occupied their minds. I understood the business challenges they were facing. Without their help, I could no longer stay and bail water from a sinking ship. With a great amount of reluctance, I gave my notice. I decided to let go of the life I had poured my soul, my sweat, my life and my devotion into and I finally, walked away.

My new co-worker listened as I told her about what had been going on there. She told me she loved what she was doing. She was helping create a Women's Educational division in new the financial company. The division would be centered on helping women entrepreneurs and other women understand and plan for their own financial needs.

My background in business development and operations made me a good candidate to join the team. I had also been through business finance classes in both my undergraduate and master's degree programs. I had self-funded the startup of my own company. I had also attended popular money classes in the community such as

Entreleadership and Financial Peace University. My new job required I take licensing tests to work in the industry. I studied and passed the tests. I was ready to start a new adventure.

2

I had a busy day scheduled with my new colleague. We had a list of things we needed to get done before we went downtown to our weekly Thursday night meeting. I grew to like being a part of a new crowd. We were a group of people working toward a common purpose. I was back to being able to help others, this time with their financial needs. The people I worked with were supportive and

---

[2] To access printable artwork visit www.everysingledaycorporation.com

passionate. A welcome change to what I endured.

Often after a long workday my new co-workers would get together to go to clubs or bars. Although I don't drink alcohol or particularly like going to clubs, I would often tag along to gain acceptance among my peers. After one extremely long day they begged me to meet up with them to try a club we hadn't been to yet. I was very tired but reluctantly agreed to meet them. I didn't want them to think I wasn't fun. In a rush to meet with them I left my ID in the car. I didn't want to go back and get it. My car was blocks and blocks away from where we were going. I decided I would charm the bouncer at the door to get in. I thought my plan was perfect.

The bouncer was big and tall. Not bad looking. My friends and I approached him. I looked up at him and said, "Hey, I forgot my ID in the car. For just this one time will you let me in? I don't even drink. I'm just going in to hang out for a bit. What do you think?" My co-workers were embarrassed at what I was asking. People didn't get into clubs or bars without an ID. Some other bar goers came out of the door laughing and talking. The bouncer was looking around as if contemplating what to do. My friend took me by the arm and said, "They can't just let you in. It's against the rules." I didn't know. I didn't frequent these places on a regular basis. The bouncer waved me over. He let me in and told me to stay out of trouble.

We walked through the door and my co-workers were immediately chatting. "I can't believe he let you in. They never do that. I think he is in to you. I don't think he would have done that for one of us." I started laughing. I really didn't think it was that big of deal I had asked nicely. I'm not a drinker so I didn't see the harm. We went down to the private basement in the club. My co-workers had a drink or two while I sat at the bar drinking my soda. When I finished my soda it was time to leave and go to another bar. This time I would have to go get my ID. When we walked out of the club the bouncer was still greeting customers at the door. I glanced over and said, "thank you." He grabbed my co-worker that was walking behind me and pulled her aside. I walked up the sidewalk before I noticed she wasn't behind me.

I leaned up against the side rail and waited for her to finish talking. After she finished talking to him she walked up to me with a big smile while laughing. "I told you he was into you!" "What are you talking about?" I asked with confusion. "He just told to me how beautiful he thinks you are. He asked me if you are married. He said 'she has to be married. There is no way a woman like that wouldn't be married'." I told him you are single and available. He gave me his business card from a non-profit company he is started. He asked me to give it to you. She leaned into my face, "he wants you to call him." I was flattered but felt shy and uncomfortable. While I was shaking my head in disbelief, we walked away. I tucked his card into my pocket and grabbed a bike taxi to take me back to get my ID so we could go to the next bar.

My co-worker called me the next morning. "What do you think about the bouncer from last night?" Oh gosh, I hadn't thought much about it. "He was totally into you." I replied, "Maybe but, I don't really think he is my type." We went on talking and she convinced me that even if I didn't think I wanted to go out with him, maybe I could offer him some financial education and potentially he could become a client. It wasn't a terrible idea as I was looking to build my client list. I decided it couldn't hurt.

In the end I gave him a call. He answered and seemed happy that I had reached out. He was very kind in telling me he hadn't ever seen anyone so beautiful and that my eyes were amazing. He mentioned that a sophisticated woman like me probably wouldn't be interested in him. I told him I didn't know what he meant and that I didn't know anything about him. I invited him to come to a free financial launch party for the new company I was working with. He agreed that it might be a good opportunity for him.

He began texting multiple times a day. He wrote many poems and sent them to me. It was really very sweet. In these types of situations, it was hard for me to know what to say. Admittedly, I had a habit of shying away from men unless they made it known they were interested in me. This was no exception. He also told me more about himself. He was very interesting to talk with. He had started a non-profit to help unprivileged kids in after school athletic programs. I really admired that about him.

A few days later after he had been texting he called me to talk. While we were talking he told me there was something he needed to tell me. I remember it very clearly. He complemented me and got right to it. He explained that he hadn't been completely honest. He let me know that he had a woman in his life. He said they had been together for many years and that he had followed her here from another state. I thought to myself… "If you have a girlfriend why are you talking to me? Why are you texting me and calling me?" By the way he was acting toward me, I never would have known he was involved with someone. It made me feel angry and confused.

I asked him to stop texting me. I asked him specifically to stop sending me poems. It wasn't fair to the woman he had in his life and if I were in her situation I would not be okay with it. A couple of weeks later he sent me a message letting me know he was moving to another state. He wasn't sure he was going to keep the same number and that ended our relationship.

Where was my dream man? Remember the guy who made my heart race every time we were together? I had a great desire to have a good, solid and healthy relationship. I usually tried to make the relationships that came into my life work, thinking I might not get another opportunity. Why was it so hard for the man of my dreams to find me or for me to find him? What was it that was keeping me from getting I wanted? It was like any dream a person may have that they just couldn't figure out how to make a reality. It was so frustrating!

I moved on with my life. I was hurting. I wasn't happy. I had no idea where my life was headed or how I ended up in the situation I was currently living. Owning a nice pretty house, with my sweet dog and living the dream of working, being single and doing whatever I wanted whenever I wanted. But I was alone, unsettled and this life didn't feel right. Something was missing. This wasn't me. I wasn't sure what was me, I started to realize I didn't know what I truly wanted or needed from life. I felt lost and it was painful. I found it hard to admit and I didn't tell anyone how I felt. I just kept working letting everyone know how great things were and how happy I was. Underneath all of the smiles and perceived happiness I was lying, I was miserable.

BRUISED

My life moved on with very few changes. I kept working at the new financial company. I attended various trainings and was invited to speak at a few of them. I had a good story. I was a young girl who grew up on a farm, went to school, had a career as an executive of a company, owned my own home, and paid cash for my Master's Degree. Some people might say I was inspiring.

On the inside I felt empty. I wasn't happy. As much as I knew I needed to leave my job at the health care company. I missed it! I missed the ease of knowing what I was doing every day. I missed being in charge and having an executive title. I missed the impressed looks I got when I told people my position. I had power. I was somebody.

So, I worked hard that summer. I wanted to be back on the top of my career again. I cut vacations I had planned short. I missed nights out with my friends. I gave up parties, watching soccer games and days at the pool to work and do more work. I was masking my pain. I was masking the hurt I was feeling of not knowing what I really wanted in life. The burning I had to find someone to marry deepened immensely. In my mind finding someone to love me and marry me would solve all the issue of not knowing what I wanted in life. Being married would mean I would always have a person, right? It meant I would never spend a weeknight or weekend alone again. It meant I would always have someone to celebrate my birthday and send me flowers on Valentine's Day. I knew marriage was the solution to my feelings of despair and uncertainty.

I also believed my husband would surely be rich or have a great job so I could stop working. I could start having a dozen babies and would be able to stay home. I would love it! Not working and taking care of kids, how hard could that really be? I had managed people and supervised them for years and years. I knew I could do it. Others had found great happiness in marriage. I believed being married would fill the empty space I had inside of me and give my life meaning. My purpose was going to be to focus on getting married.

How exactly does one focus on getting married? I told myself it meant that I needed to be skinny. I always carried extra weight. I grew up chubby. In my adult years, I started exercising more and would sometimes eat healthy. I knew guys would like me better if I were skinny so that was the first step. Next, I wanted to make sure I wasn't holding onto anything in my past.

My heart mourned. There were a few men who had come into my life with whom I felt a great connection. I felt loved, honored and cherished in certain moments with them. In two of my most genuine relationships in my life the men hadn't been honest with me. They were either seeing other women behind my back or lying to me about other aspects of their lives. I grieved the loss of companionship. I felt naïve and I resented that I could be so blind to someone lying to me. I had scars and deep trust issues. I didn't really know how to deal with them.

I went to see my great friend and hair stylist. I had a burning desire to let go of things I felt like I was holding onto in my past. I decided one thing I could do with little effort was to cut my hair. When I told my friend I wanted her to chop off all of my hair she asked me if I were sure. I was definitely sure about this. I hoped the haircut would inspire a new attitude about not being completely happy with my life.

While she cut my hair, I shared details with her about what had been happening. She already knew I changed jobs. She had known me for years. She already knew about my sadness and the deepest desires of my heart. She was one person I knew I could trust. She told me about an intuitive energy healer she had been working with. She said the healer had been very good at helping her discover and work through some things in her past. It seemed like something I might want to consider. I asked for her phone number.

When my haircut was finished and she turned me around in the chair to see the transformation, I screamed out loud with excitement and tears came to my eyes. I loved it! The haircut was perfect for me! The style and color breathed newness and adventure into my eyes. I couldn't believe the change it created in my face and in my heart. I hugged my friend tightly and thanked her for being such an important part of my life and for helping me feel beautiful.

one of the HARDEST things you will EVER HAVE TO DO is GRIEVE the LOSS OF A PERSON who is still ALIVE!

[3]

A few days after getting my new hairdo I called the energy healer and made an appointment. The day of my appointment with the energy healer I felt all kinds of nerves. I had seen therapists before but this was different. I didn't know what to expect. It can be uncomfortable to think that you are going to divulge your secrets to a complete stranger and they are going to help you through it. I had financial appointments with clients scheduled for that day. I was also meeting up with some new work mates for training later that evening.

---

[3] To access printable artwork visit www.everysingledaycorporation.com

The only way I was going to be able to have the appointment with the healer was over the phone. We were not going to be able to meet in person. She called me at the time we had set up. I was sitting in an office downtown Salt Lake City. I had exactly one hour to talk with her before my next appointment.

After a brief introduction she asked me what my intention was for the session. I was shaking a little and my voice was weak. I explained to her that I wanted to know if my heart was broken. I told her that there were a few relationships from my past that I didn't think I was over. That all I really wanted in my life was to be married. I told her I wanted to clear out any blocks that might be in my heart or my mind so that I could move forward. I also told her I had just switched jobs and that I doubted my decision. I just needed help. I wanted help moving forward and finding happiness.

She walked me through a heart opening exercise to my calm my mind and open up my heart. She could tell me my heart wasn't broken. My heart was just badly bruised. The most interesting part of the session was that my heart wasn't bruised from the men I had been in relationships with in my past. The bruise was from something in my childhood.

I had been carrying it with me for a very long time. The years in my childhood that came to my mind were the ages of six and eight. During this process, I was in a meditative state. The healer had asked me to picture in my mind the most comfortable place in my life. It was my newly remodeled bedroom. I pictured myself sitting on my perfectly comfortable bed. My six-year-old self asked if she could come in and talk with me.

With my heart racing I said yes. The healer walked me through inviting my young self to sit down with my adult self on my bed. Growing up my family gave me the nickname Annie. I'm not sure if it was because I loved the old-time movie Annie with Daddy Warbucks or if it was because my real name ended with Ann. Regardless, in my meditation I called my young self, Annie. She asked me how young Annie was feeling. I explained that she was sad; she felt scared and was lonely. She felt like she didn't have anyone to love her. As I heard myself repeating these words out loud my heart started to ache so deeply for my young childhood self. Tears began to seep out of my eyes and roll down my face. I hadn't realized my emotions of loneliness and the feelings of not being loved extended back to when I was six years old.

I was born into a kind and loving family. When I was young we worked hard and we had a lot of responsibilities. My dad had taken over the family farm for my grandparents. I was provided for and given shelter. Despite these things, I didn't feel loved and my heart was sad. The energy healer asked me about my spiritual beliefs. Meaning did I believe in a spiritual being like God a creator or did I believe in Karma or the Energy of the Universe or Science. I told her my belief was in God the Eternal Father.

Once I gave her this direction she asked if I believed in Jesus Christ as a Savior and I said yes. She asked me if I would be willing to let the Savior come and heal my heart. At this point, I could barely speak. Tears and heartache were overwhelming me. I agreed to allow the Savior to come to me. I changed the scenery in my mind and switched to a beautiful mountain meadow where my

Savior walked beside me. Young Annie was there with me, walking along, holding my hand. Both of us were dressed in white.

The Savior showed me the nail prints in His hands. Without speaking I knew He had suffered for my grief. He knew the heartache I was feeling. As we sat in the meadow I felt that the Savior wanted to take away my pain. But I had to let Him. I had to give Him permission and allow the pain and heartache I was carrying to be lifted. He would leave it there if I decided I wanted it. He would allow me to hold it if I felt I needed it to continue to mold and shape my life.

It was my choice, my heart, my journey and my pain. I didn't want to keep it. I wanted newness, hope and understand. As tears continued to fall from my face I gave permission. As I allowed my spirit to release the hurt and the loneliness, peace began to rush over my body. My skin had goose bumps, my heart was racing and the hairs on my arms were standing on end. The cleansing tears of letting go were starting to cease; my mind and heart began to feel lighter. My soul started to feel happy.

Once I allowed the Savior to take my burden I felt light and free. I felt my heart pumping in my own chest. I felt it pounding as if it were big and bold and vibrant. The healer continued to talk with me. She spoke about angels around me, protecting me and guiding me. We talked of my grandparents who had passed away and the pride they felt for me. She said that I had been born with certain gifts. All people are born with their own set of special gifts. She explained that my life had great meaning and that multitudes of people were waiting for me. Remembering that we had never met face to face nor had seen pictures of each other she said that people saw heaven in my eyes.

With that statement, our appointment ended. I had a meeting I needed to get to. Work associates were waiting for me at the door. I thanked the energy healer graciously and humbly for her time, her energy and her willingness to share her gifts with others. I felt amazing!! The absolute best I had felt in years. I wasn't a broken person. I didn't have a broken heart. I could proudly walk tall and boldly know that I had value. I had worth. I could move forward. Yeah! Yeah! Yeah! I was frantic with excitement. In the space of a one-hour phone call my life was different. My heart felt lighter. I was no longer bruised, I was healing and changing.

CONFIDENCE

There was a fire in my mind, my heart and my soul. I felt
as though I could conquer anything. I became more
involved in work. I felt better about life and what I was
doing. My heart was being stitched back together from the
things of my past. I was going to be able to move forward
with my life and continue to help people. An acquaintance
I knew, Nancy, who lived in California, just released a
guide called Keys to Confidence. Her guide was the
preliminary step to opening The Center of Confidence,
which she owns and operates.

I invited her to come visit. I wanted her to come and
share her confidence program with me and other women I
invited. Anyone who felt open to receive change and
abundance in their lives was welcome. It was an amazing
idea. It was right in line with the healing session I had with
the energy healer. I felt complete happiness that so many
tools were surfacing in my life to help catapult me forward.

The Keys to Confidence program would provide a step-by-step process to help me let go of emotional baggage. My baggage consisted of feeling alone, sad and directionless. I knew my heart wasn't broken. It was time to work on other things I had been feeling. The program would also help others let go of the baggage they were carrying. It would teach us how to set intentions to move forward with purpose and confidence. Nancy arrived the day before the Keys to Confidence program was scheduled. I picked her up at the airport with great excitement.

As we were driving to lunch I began sharing some of the things that had been happening in my life. I felt comfortable sharing with her the amazing session I had with the energy healer and the things I had learned about my past. When I mentioned to Nancy that I had met with an energy healer, Nancy revealed that she was also a healer. I was stunned that another energy healer was showing up in my life. The thought washed over me and settled into my heart with contentment.

Nancy and I laughed and talked over lunch. We ran a few errands to grab some items we needed for the Keys to Confidence program the next day. We met with some of my co-workers that night and then went back to my place to get some sleep before the big event the following morning. It was exhilarating to have Nancy stay with me. She was open and honest. I loved being able to talk with her about all of the new ideas and inspirations I was learning. We stayed up late into the night talking and went to bed just hours before we needed to wake up to get to the program.

As I woke up the next morning, the first thing I saw

out of the corner of eye in my bedroom was a giant spider.
I let out a little yelp and went out of my room to grab a
tissue. Nancy asked me what I was doing. I frantically told
her there was a gigantic spider in my bedroom. She
jumped up and yelled for me not to kill it. She explained to
me that spiders had great energy. I hadn't heard of this
before.

They were thought to be an insect that could bring an
intention back to you. If you think about it, spiders find a
home, spin a web to attract what they want and then sit
and patiently wait for it. She said that if I caught the spider
and released it into the world speaking or thinking
something I desired to have in my life the universe would
start working to bring that desire back to me.

It couldn't hurt to catch the spider and release it. I
was in the new found high from my energy healing session
a few weeks ago. I gently nudged the spider into the tissue.
Although it grossed me out I walked quietly to my back
yard and released the spider. As I put her down in my
flowerbed I sent the great intention of my heart into the
world. I asked the spider to bring my family to me. I was
thinking to myself go little spider bring them into my life.

Nancy and I finished getting ready and headed down
to the meeting for the Keys to Confidence program. For
the program, we were asked to bring a notepad or journal.
This was to be a place where we could write down our
thoughts and impressions. As Nancy walked us through
different meditations, and insights into the power of words
and the power of our intentions my faith in the power of
our minds began to increase.

She demonstrated to us the impact certain words
have in our lives and our attitudes. Negative words and

harsh words literally carry a negative energy with them when they are spoken. Loving and kind words have the same impact on our hearts and minds in a positive way. She explained how any self-hate, shame or guilt we think impacts us negatively. Judgments we have on ourselves and on others create the same negativity. Whether they are thought or spoken. This instruction seemed natural to me. Of course, words have power but I hadn't necessarily accepted that they had energy. It was a piece of wisdom I was happy to hold on to.

We meditated on our lives during the program. We were asked to think of the time in our life when we felt the happiest. We also listed the time in our life when we felt the deepest sadness and a time when we had experienced the most anger. The purpose of this exercise was to help us understand that every experience and emotion is meant for our learning, development and growth. It is meant to provide instruction and enable us to face and process our emotions. Emotions that at times we feel may bury us. Other emotions of joy we want to hold onto forever. It is important for us to be able to accept and understand all emotion. It was an amazing experience to reflect and define those moments. We truly can see the goodness in all things if we allow our hearts and minds to be centered and focused on our complete journey not just that one suffocating or exhilarating moment.

We came to a section in the program where we were invited to do a visualization of letting go of burdens or baggage we were carrying. Any negative thought or feeling we were holding. My experience with the energy healer was similar. Nancy walked us through sitting on a beach with a beautiful vista. A quiet breeze was blowing and no one else was around us. We were alone on the beach. She gently encouraged us to pack up things we were holding that caused us sadness, darkness or grief. In the visualization, we placed these items in a bowl, walked into the ocean until the water was at waste level and let go of the bowl. We allowed our bowl holding our sadness or pain to be carried away. We watched them until they disappeared out of sight. In Nancy's wisdom, she helped us release these burdens and, let them flow out of our lives. My heart and soul were feeling more and more free.

In my vision of burdens, I saw my previous employment. The job as a Vice President I had so dearly held on to. Working, as an executive wasn't bad, the situation I found myself in was what caused my grief. At the end it brought a lot of miscommunication and feelings that I had no value. I watched it float away. I watched the sadness I felt during the last years I had been employed there leave me. I started letting go. My process was beginning.

One of the next steps in Nancy's Keys to Confidence program.[4] Was to learn about self-affirmations. I had never spoken an affirmation in my life. We were given individual hand-held mirrors. As we looked in to our own eyes we repeated statements about our beauty, our strength, our instinct and our divinity. We had to repeat the words aloud, together three times while looking into the mirrors. About half way through the second time of repeating the affirmations I began to cry. I couldn't hold it in any longer. The energy of the message and releasing the burdens from my life had gotten to me. My eyes bubbled with tears. I couldn't stop them from rolling down my cheeks. I was

[4] For more about Key to Confidence visit www.everysingleday corporation.com

feeling the power of the words as I said them to myself. Loving words, kind words, and positive words. Additional words such as strength, valor and purpose. As I was saying them, I began to allow myself to believe them. My heart felt a peaceful rhythm of love, understanding and purpose. I was changing. I could feel it.

I finished the program with so much hope and joy and freedom. I was indescribably grateful to Nancy. I was grateful for her example and her confidence. I valued her willingness to step into her light as a mentor and a healer.

My perception of life was beginning to be very different. I started mapping out possibilities of what I might create with the things I was learning about healing, intentions, the universe and the power of positive thinking. I loved learning how to set things free from my life. I began to use the meditation often to release feelings of disappointment or failed expectations. I started wondering to myself about the possibilities of intentions.

I reasoned in my mind that if I could meditate to release negative things from my life it would be possible to use meditation to bring positive things into my life. I didn't see the down side of testing my theory. I wanted to test the possibility of bringing things into my life. Before I did my experiment with positive intentions I thought about a few things I wanted.

As far as work was going for me, I had been able to help some people with their finances but it wasn't going to be enough to sustain me long term. I knew there were great possibilities out there; I just needed them to come to me. I decided that I wanted to set an intention to get more clients. The other intention I wanted was for a man to come into my life. As I sat to focus and go through my positive intentions meditation I pictured myself on a beach with a man. I put no judgment on the image I was seeing. I let my mind be free and the image of a man came clearly into my mind. I pictured us holding hands and laughing. We played in the ocean and were both very happy. During the meditation I also pictured some children with us. I then switched my meditation to gaining more clients to help with their finances. I allowed myself to envision meeting with them and growing in my experience as a wealth planner.

A few weeks later, to my surprise, the intentions I had set came into my life. They came within a few days of each other. The first manifestation was finding some additional clients. As part of my training with the financial company it was common to start conversations with people as I was out in public doing the things in my regular life. One day I had decided to go into a locally owned shopped on Main Street in the city I lived in. I quickly became friends with the owner. I started telling him a little bit about my life and explained to him that I worked in the financial industry as a wealth planner. He said back to me, "I have been looking for someone to review some of my accounts. I am getting close to retirement and want to get a second opinion on what might be some good options for me. Would you be willing to take a look for me?" I was elated. Of course I would review his accounts.

After I set up a time to meet back with him I walked across the street to talk with the business owner of an accounting firm. We were already acquainted. We began chatting and I also told him I was working in the finance industry helping people with wealth planning. He told me he had a client come to him just a few days before that needed help working out some investments. He asked if I would be willing to give them a review. I couldn't believe what was happening. I felt as if I was living in a dream. I was happy to help. I was stunned to realize my positive intention meditations had worked. I had drawn into my life two potential new clients. The positive momentum it gave me was very fun!

5

I was happily going through my life and living day to day. My dog needed some medication. I decided to run over to my vet's office to pick it up. When I got to

[5] To access printable artwork visit www.everysingledaycorporation.com

Veterinarian office it was closed for lunch but would be opening again in 15 minutes. There was a gas station across the street. I had never been there before but I needed gas. I decided to drive across the street to fill up my gas tank and grab a drink.

I was standing outside my car enjoying the warm summer sun thinking about my new clients and how life was moving in my favor and how amazing it felt to be in control. The gas pump clicked indicating my tank was full. Once I was back in my car I heard someone lightly honk. I looked around and there was a man in a big white truck pulling a cattle trailer waving through his window at me. I waved and pointed forward that I was done. He started to roll down his window and I did the same. I said, "I am done you can have the pump". He stuttered and said "uh no, I actually just wanted to talk to you. How are you doing?"

He continued to talk to me for a few more minutes. He said that he noticed me and thought I was very pretty. He was wondering if he might be able to call me sometime. Really? Was he serious? This was fascinating to me. The memory of the intentions I set came to my mind. Who was I to judge what was happening. I had a couple of business cards sitting in my car console. I grabbed one, jumped out of my car and walked over to his truck. As I walked over, I noticed he had similar features to the man I had imagined in my intention meditation. He asked me if I was married. I told him that no, I wasn't married. He rambled, "How could someone like you not be married. You have an amazing presence about you. I'm shocked." His comments and flattery made me feel amazing. But, I did always feel a tinge of sadness when someone asked why I wasn't married. Without meaning to, it made me feel like a failure because I wasn't married. Most of the time I had no idea how to respond to this question. I didn't know why I wasn't married. My programmed response was usually, "I guess I just haven't found the right person for me to marry."

He told me that he thought he might be too old for me. He said he had three kids and the oldest was 19. He told me he owned a ranch and had just been to buy some new cattle. I responded that I had grown up in a small farm in Northern Utah. I had an understanding about cattle. The conversation was natural and flowed easily. I handed him my business card and told him I was a wealth planner. He asked if it would be okay to call me. I told him "Sure. Why not?"

I left the gas station and finally got over to the vet's office. I was driving home to get some work done when my phone began to ring. It wasn't a number I recognized. I didn't answer and the caller didn't leave a voicemail. Ten minutes later my phone rang again. The same number, I didn't answer, no voicemail. A few minutes later, the same number again. I answered with a quiet Hello. "Oh hi, this is the guy from the gas station. I just thought I would call while I am driving to chat with you some more. Do you have a few minutes?" If there was one thing I could give the guy credit for it was he being forward and confident. I had nothing to lose and was feeling brave so I stayed on the phone.

He said he had never done anything like that before. He said he felt drawn to me. He told me again that he thought he was too old. I asked him to tell me his age. He said he was 50. I told him I was 37, which was a 13-year difference. I felt indifferent to the difference in our ages. Then he shared something I wasn't expecting, "Well, I should let you know that I am technically married." That was interesting. In my opinion, a married person generally shouldn't tell someone they are pretty and ask for their phone number. My perception is that this was not okay. He explained to me that he and his wife were separated and hadn't been living together for almost a year. It might be okay with some people if a person who is separated from a spouse seeks a dating opportunity, but for me, I didn't think it was right.

So, I had to wonder about the intention I set. I did believe the intention of bringing a man into my life had worked. But, I was new at this; my intention setting experiment needed some work. I had asked for a man to come into my life. A man indeed came into my life. Maybe I wasn't clear though; I wanted a man I could marry to come into my life, not a married man to come into my life. I would have to keep working on this.

What I had learned through this process was that it was possible to bring things into our lives through meditation and setting intentions. The other thing I learned was that I had some strong issues resurfacing about not being married and the judgments I felt others placing on me for not being married.

The voices in my head started speaking immediately, Why does this happen? Why don't any single, available men like me? Why couldn't I just attract a normal, single, available man? I knew that not everyone had the same issue I did of not being able to find someone to marry But there are so many things that each of us face that are trying.

For some it may be a long sought for career or vocation opportunity. For others it might be not being able to have children or to grow their family. It could be a child or a family member who has an issue or difficult illness. It could be mental or physical challenges. It could be the same thing or a completely different thing for each of us. For me it was marriage. All I could think was why is this the one thing eluding me? What was wrong with me?

It was the hardest truth to face and truly made me believe there was something wrong with me. Something I was doing wasn't good enough. I was too tall, I wasn't skinny enough, I was too independent, and I was too smart or too dumb. I didn't like enough sports. I was too timid or maybe too extreme. On and on and on, self-pity and loathing at its finest. It was exhausting.

I talked on the phone with the guy from the gas station a few more times. He mentioned to me that he had some money he wanted to move for his kids. I believed I could help him with his finances so I kept answering when he called. But when he called, he either wanted to chat to see how I was doing or put feelers out to see if I would have lunch with him. The answer was no. I wasn't going to have lunch with him. He was married. Eventually I stopped answering his phone calls and he stopped calling me.

After all this I regressed to my safe reaction and I stopped thinking about finding someone to marry. I focused on work, building my client list and on losing more unwanted pounds. Even with the healing work I had processed in the last couple of week, the same old thought crept into my mind; I wasn't the type of girl that got married. I put back on my masks of loving my job and my house and that I was so happy to hide my insecurities. I didn't know how to solve it. I didn't want to try and set any new intentions at this point. My newly found confidence and healing were beginning to waver.

ADMITTANCE

Now, I had these two potential new clients that were good prospects to grow my financial clientele. I had a lot to be grateful for. I wanted to give these new clients my best. I was relatively nervous about being able to help them with their needs. I had only been working in this industry for a few months. I had an adequate amount of confidence in myself. I believed that I successfully managed my personal finances. I paid cash for my Master's degree and cash for my beautiful home remodel. I had no debts other than my house payment and funded the startup of my own waffle catering company.

I believed the decision to leave my twelve-year career in health care was the right path. I no longer went to an office every day, which was nice. I was working a lot of hours but if I wanted to meet a friend for lunch I could. I had somewhat of a free schedule. I kept telling myself, life was great.

Because these new clients wanted special types of account, I knew I needed help. I called our back-end office and spent several hours on the phone reviewing account possibilities and options. I spoke to leaders in our company and got their advice on how to structure each client's wealth plan. I put together spreadsheets and Word documents listing their options. I spent a lot of time preparing to meet with each of them. I really wanted to gain their business. Although, I didn't understand everything I thought I was ready.

I set up a meeting with the first client. He had a special case and would need to provide a large sum of money for the initial investment. As I provided the information and explained in detail the great outcome of what my recommended investment would yield, I started to get an insecure vibe. I started having major doubts. The client said they would review the information and get back to me. In a panic, I offered to have them meet with an executive agent to answer any additional questions. I wanted the client to know I was putting their needs first and I wanted them to have the absolute best. Really, I was trying to hide my insecurities and the real truth that I started to admit to myself was that I didn't like working in finance. There were a few things they asked that I didn't know the answer to. I was still very much a rookie. I worked on staying in a positive mindset. I meditated and told myself that I needed to release what I was holding on to. The negative momentum was starting to crash me.

I pulled myself together and went to meet with the other new client. I had several options ready to present. I pulled information on a number of accounts and options. I thought having options was good. There were different types of accounts that provided different benefits. This was going to be fantastic. As I sat down and proceeded to present the options, I could sense they were not impressed. I realized that I had missed the mark during our first meeting. This client was looking for simplicity. Too many choices were just too many choices. I needed to use my understanding to advise them on what to do not give them choices.

I was excited my positive intentions had come into my life. But, I failed to realize I might have gotten in over my head with the financial clients. After a few more reviews and meetings, both clients decided to not work with me. I began to ponder this deeply. I do believe subconsciously they both picked up on my insecure energy. I had set my intentions from what my mind wanted but my heart was not connected to wanting those things. The intentions came into my life and left just as quickly. All the doubt I was feeling about not knowing what I was doing started flying through my mind like the wind before a tornado.

Something didn't feel right. I started reflecting over my experiences of the last few months. I healed some deep things from my childhood. I released the sadness I felt about leaving my job in the health care industry. Both of those things felt amazing. Since I started working through those things it became easier for me to recognize when something in my life wasn't right. At this point, I started realizing it was working as a wealth planner. It wasn't the right fit for me. I had been trying to make it work but it wasn't working.

The investment accounts I dealt with at the financial company were good, great even. I studied and understood them well. I just didn't feel passionate about it. In reality, it hadn't quite been what I thought it would be. It wasn't the company's fault. It was just different than my initial understanding. I had a very stable career up until this point in my life. I was feeling so unsettled. I was used to having control over my life and what has happening. I was letting go of many things and it was causing everything to shift.

I thought about the spider I caught in my bedroom. I also thought about the intentions I had set. They were the beginning of some great beliefs. We do have the power to create scenarios in our lives. We have the instinctual nature to know when something is not right. I was starting to grasp these concepts and understand them.

In my heart I felt like my life was an illusion. In the eyes of society, friends and family I had everything going for me. I had a good job and a good education. I traveled to exotic places and made good money. I owned my own home. I was able to do the things I wanted to. Many people didn't have this luxury. I felt very guilty for not being grateful for it at this moment. What more was there in the world to provide greater fulfillment other than to have a family.

I felt like I should be complete. I should have been happy and joyful. But, I wasn't. The hard truth was that I knew my life was meant to be more. Inside of me, in my inner spirit there was more. It was blossoming; I could feel my mindset changing. My job in the financial industry became less and less exciting and fulfilling to me. I wasn't reaching my full potential. I had only been employed with the company for six months. I knew there was always a learning curve to a new job especially with a new company but this was different. I was trying to get people to care about their finances as much as I did, and to be honest most people just didn't. It's one of those things where either you are a freak about it or you don't even acknowledge it exists.

at any given moment YOU HAVE THE POWER TO say: THIS iS NOT HOW THE STORY iS GOING TO END

[6]

I had taken the position at the financial company believing I would be a part of a great movement to change people's lives and have purpose again. The company wasn't growing at the rate I thought it would. The woman's division was taking more time than I expected to get started. Ultimately, I knew I didn't want do this long

[6] To access printable artwork visit www.everysingledaycorporation.com

term. I didn't know exactly how to get out of it. My pride wasn't wanting me to admit I was in the wrong industry and career for me.

UNSETTLED

Months after I left my job in health care, I was looking at being unemployed. I felt like a failure. My pride was being destroyed. I had to work. I needed to be doing something. I didn't want to go back to working in health care. I had no idea what I wanted to do. I didn't know how to figure it out on my own. Inspiration came that I should make another appointment with the energy healer. Maybe, there was another scenario from my past that was keeping me for knowing what to do. I sent her a text and set up an appointment.

A week later I met with the energy healer. This time we met in person. The moment I saw her, we connected. Her disposition and character were soft and welcoming. I felt immediate peace in my heart when I sat down with her. As was customary, she asked me what my intentions were for the session. I explained to her that I felt a little stuck in my life. I spoke about my work situation and how I left a really good job to work in a new industry but that I was unhappy and didn't know what my next step should be. She asked if there were anything else. Unexpectedly, I began crying, my heart knew what I had been hiding, the thing I tried to bury. It was always there, the underlying desire of everything. All I really wanted was to be married.

I just wanted to have "my person". The one person in the world who was obligated to love me, listen to me, support me and help me make hard decisions. I wanted to have children that I could serve and nurture. I wanted security knowing they loved me. I poured my heart out to her about my deepest tender desires. I was sobbing. While explaining how badly I wanted a family and children, she listened empathetically. She repeated back to me what she was hearing. That I wanted to be married and have children because I thought it would provide automatic love and security. I agreed that was what I wanted.

She then asked me a simple but pivotal question, "How do you know marriage and children will provide those things?" I didn't know I just thought they would. Then she said, "Do you believe it is possible that there are married people who don't feel those things?" For sure, I thought that was true. "Then why would your marriage undoubtedly provide those things? What makes you special or unique?" As I said the words, I knew they were false, "Because I have waited so long to get married, I deserved those things." I laugh at myself now. Who was I to deserve more than another person? Years of waiting and working made me no more qualified to have an abundant, loving marriage than any other person. Life was work. Married, single, divorced, a widower, life was work, having love in your life regardless of your circumstance was based on acknowledgement and striving for it every day not because in your mind you felt like you deserved it.

She continued using a great example "Laurann", she said, "Your future self is torturing your present self. It is holding a carrot in front of you saying here is marriage, here is your dream, come and get it I dare you. Your past self is crippling you by telling you aren't thin enough, or pretty enough." Ahhhhhh! She was right. There were so many voices telling me why I couldn't get married and the thing I wanted most in life was evading me.

She walked me through an exercise that allowed me to live in the present moment. The past was the past and the future wasn't here yet. If I could focus my mind on each current moment I would be able let go of my endless list of expectations and start actually living. I wouldn't have to worry about how and when I would have a husband. I would be centered on the now of my life instead of the when of my life.

She had me close my eyes. I took a deep breath and exhaled. Then I placed my hand over my heart. I could feel my heart beating in my chest I took another deep breath. She explained God, lives in this moment. When you stop and focus on the moment, your mind must stop its ramblings and worries and is in this exact moment. This is where God exists in each moment, as it happens, not in the future, not in the past. Right here, with you, watching over you, understanding you, knowing you. This is where you find peace.

there's something MAGICAL about a person who is FULLY GROUNDED —in the— PRESENT MOMENT

I had chills all over my body. He was there. I could feel His presence. I knew Him. He loved me. He was so proud of me. I am His daughter. Nothing I do will take that away or change it. My father, my God, loved me. I opened my eyes with tears streaming down my face.

Energy of peace and contentment can be created through many different forms of meditation or stillness. My belief in God, the Creator of the Universe, allows me to feel comfort and security. Other people may feel this through means of worship, meditation or speaking with a religious or spiritual leader. Others find this sense of direction by being in nature, fishing on a boat, running in

---

[7] To access printable artwork visit www.everysingledaycorporation.com

the hills, kayaking down a river or through other personal means of connection. It is all a matter of understanding what method most resonates with you. Then learning to master and honor that method.

The question of what I should do with my life was still swirling in my mind. We decided to do a deeper meditation. Meditation can also be consider a prayer. Both are a form of letting your thoughts and concerns be heard to receive answers. The purpose of the meditation was to allow me to practice the concept of finding answers for myself without the need of a healer.

The meditation I choose was to ask the Savior his advice on what I needed to do and how I could be comforted. The moments I spend with my Savior are very quiet, sacred, and personal to me. I put my hand over my heart again and closed my eyes. I pictured the Savior in my mind. While breathing slowly and listening to the beat of my heart I asked him if I could talk with him. I felt his presence come into the room. I knew I could talk with Him and tell Him all of the things that were bothering me.

Sitting in the quiet, comfortable room, I felt the love and acceptance of my Savior. I felt His love. I felt His concern, His patience, His empathy. In my thoughts I poured out my desire to get married, my desire to have love and security in my life. I also asked for advice on what I should to do about working. I told Him I wasn't happy working in the financial industry and that I had a distinct feeling it wasn't the right path for me. As I sat there contemplating these thoughts one very distinct impression came to my mind. An impression that shocked me. The direction was that I needed to sell my home. I couldn't believe this was what I was feeling. I loved my house. I put my entire heart into my home. My beautiful remodeled, perfectly suited for me home. The home I found security and solace in for nearly nine years. My gathering place, my solitude, my beacon of success and accomplishment.

Few things in my life had ever been so clear. I knew I had to do it. I timidly opened my eyes and looked up, "I need to sell my home." She gently smiled at me. She knew I was on the path of change. A path of healing and becoming someone different, someone new. I can't describe the relief I felt. As the inspiration seeped into my bones, I knew this was my next step. I didn't know why or where I was headed but I knew it was time. It was the beginning of a new journey. Selling my home would allow me time to settle my thoughts and my mind. It would also allow me to disconnect from the material things I used for security. I was going to be able to learn the true value of my life without the distraction of things. The inspiration to leave the financial company came as well. I was relieved.

Because I had mentioned not being happy at my job, the healer mentioned an opportunity about working with an idea management company that she had recently come across. They helped people explore and understand ideas about creating a business. They only worked on a referral basis. She was only allowed to send them two referrals during a certain period of time.

She wanted to give me one of the referrals. The referral came in the form of a business card with only an email address. I was to send an email to the address on the card stating my interest in setting up a meeting. The company would contact me for an interview time. My mind and spirit were excited and nervous for the next part in my journey.

FIVE BILLION

The energy I walked away with from the healing session stayed with me for days. I drove home from the appointment in silence. I didn't turn on the radio or hook up the auxiliary cable to my iPhone. I wanted to let the truths I discovered settle into my mind. I arrived home and pulled into my garage thinking to myself with very profound conviction I am going to sell my home. I was also going to quit working with the financial company and email the idea management company. Those three ideas were going to change world a lot of things in my world.

I felt more drawn to get these done than I had felt about anything in a very long time. As I entered my home from my garage I walked slowly up the hallway through my TV room and up the stairs. I was repeating the words in my mind; I'm going to sell my house. I'm going to sell this house. For years I had been concerned about what I would do with my house if I got married. I surely wouldn't want to sell my house it was beautiful. I was more emotionally, spiritually and physically attached to my home as a sense of security than I realized. Now, within the course of an afternoon, I was settling into the thought of letting it go.

The best way for me to accept the idea of letting everything go was to set things in motion. I knew a few realtors and choose one to contact. I let him know I was looking at to sell my house. We set up an appointment for me to go to his office the following day to run some numbers on pricing, market value, condition of the home, etc. This was huge! As I took this first step toward putting my house on the market, I felt nothing but excitement. I couldn't believe how ready I was to make this happen.

Following through on the inspiration other I received I during my healing session, I sent an email to the idea management group. I sat down and wrote; "I was given this email address an energy healer you work with. My name is Laurann Turner. I want help understanding my true passion and path of life. I want to be impactful and do amazing things. My contact information is provided below." I checked over the email one more or maybe three more times. I added my contact information at the bottom and pushed send. Whoosh. That was done. I was a little terrified. I had no idea what I was getting myself into but it felt right, it felt necessary for my progression. That was all I was being led by at this moment, I had to do my part and let the rest happen.

Next I contacted the owner of the financial company where I worked. He had felt that I was distancing myself from the company. After the two new clients chose other options I became disenchanted by the opportunity. I explained to him that I didn't feel like this course of work was going to be sustainable for me any longer. He said he had plans for me to step forward as a leader in the company. He wanted me to help lead a team in the city I lived. The caveat was that, I wouldn't receive any additional compensation for doing so. The only means to making a living was a commission-based structure. I wouldn't receive any benefits to step-up as a leader. In essence, the only thing it would do is take more of my time, more energy and more effort. That was exactly what I didn't want.

I had spent years of my life working and doing that exact thing. Working hard, being a leader, making sure things got done with little additional compensation. That is what made me feel undervalued. I wasn't going to do it. Not again, not for the second time. I thanked him and let him know I was flattered but not interested. We came to an agreement; I would continue to offer support to my current clients as long as my licenses were valid. Otherwise, I would be taking a step back and allowing space for me to be open to other ventures.

I felt great. The burden of working at a place that wasn't fulfilling was gone. This was another aspect in my life I didn't realize was making me so unhappy. I had been working to work, working because I had to, working because it was expected.

I could feel a new energy coming into my life. At the time, I wasn't sure exactly what was happening but I knew it felt good. It felt awesome. I felt happy, relieved and excited for what was happening, and what was going to come. For the first time in almost a decade I felt full of life. I was starting to feel the real essence of what it felt like to be genuinely happy.

An email reply came back from the idea management company. It felt like a step in the right direction of possibly figuring out what I wanted to do. They suggested a time for us to meet. We were set to meet on a Saturday afternoon.

Two weeks prior to receiving this email I met with my realtor to review the details of selling my home. He ran comparable properties in my area. We went over the detailed listing of my home and discussed the process if I decided to sell. It was a lot to take in. The decision wasn't just if I would sell my home. It wasn't just to move to another place because I didn't like this one. It was a decision to live my life without knowing my future. It was the last remaining thing in my life that I had been clinging to for comfort and security.

It was my first home. My sweat and tears where infused in the walls, the floors, and the rooms. This place was entirely and completely me. The decision before me was a decision to change. It was a decision to relinquish control. It was a decision to trust, hope and believe. I asked my realtor if I could have one day to think about it. The same question came to my mind again, what on earth was I doing? What was my plan for my life? I honestly had no clue. I had no plans. For the first time in my short mortal life I had no plan for what came next. However, I was going to sell my home. It was my next step. It was the right thing for me. I needed change. I craved change and wanted change in my life.

I awoke the next day and within a few hours sent a text to my realtor. I was ready to do it. I was going to put my house on the market and see what happened. The next couple of days were busy. Papers to complete and sign. I needed to clean and straighten a few things. Pictures for the listing were taken, the lawn was mowed, and things were thrown away.

My home went on the market on Thursday. Within a couple of hours a few showings of the home were scheduled. We received two offers on the house after the first two showings with more showings scheduled. Amidst all of this, I was meeting with the idea management group the same weekend. Life was busy. I also decided I was going to sell most of my furniture when I moved. I didn't know where I was going to move but I did know I would be downsizing and there wouldn't be room for all my belongings. I didn't know if other people would want my things, but I wanted to sell them anyway. I decided to let my family have first dibs on anything they might want. I sent them pictures and also posted pictures on a Facebook online yard sale.

Surprisingly people wanted my things and were willing to come get them immediately. I wasn't quite ready for that. I didn't know they would sell so quickly. I told most of the people they needed to give me a week. I still had showings on the house scheduled and my meeting with the idea management group. I was far too prideful at that point in my life to allow people into my home with no furniture.

The realtor and I reviewed the offers we received on my home. After a thoughtful discussion we decided to accept one. I felt good about it. Two gentlemen came from the idea management company to meet with me. Let me remind you, I didn't know exactly what the idea management group did, I only knew that they worked in Idea Management for people who were exploring their own business ideas.

They were very kind as I greeted them. Charlie gave them a warning sniff test. Luckily for them, they passed, or things would have gotten uncomfortable fast. They began explaining to me the set-up of their company. There were different tiers and methods of discovery they helped people work through. The purpose was to determine your motivation in life and to help determine your most prominent business idea or ideas. It was all very intriguing to me. Once they explained what they did they started asking me more about me.

[8]

Well, at that moment didn't do anything as far as work. I had just quit my job with the financial company where I had only worked with for six months. Prior to that I had worked in the healthcare industry for twelve years but had also walked away. Deep inside, I felt a little unsure of what to tell them. However, the ego inside of me jumped forward and took the lead. There was no way I wasn't going to make myself sound impressive. I rattled off several of my secular accomplishments. The highlight reel included some things I've mentioned in the book so far with a little more detail. I was previously employed Vice President of a multi-million dollar national health care company; I had a Master's Degree in Business, a Bachelor's degree in Health Administration and was owner of a specialty Waffle Catering Company, and a personal S-Corporation. Most recently a Wealth Planner at a startup financial company. I was full of pride and beaming.

I felt like it was a pretty good. They complimented me on my accomplishments. They were gauging me. Watching how I reacted to questions. I wasn't prepared for the next thing they asked me. "If I had five-billion dollars what would I do with it and if I had ninety days to live, what would I do?" Geez, five-billion dollars was a lot of money. The first thought that came into my mind was to help my family. I wanted to make sure they were financially secure. I would help them pay off debts, build new homes, or care for whatever needs they might have. Then, I would give the rest of the money away. I didn't know exactly what I would do. They added the condition that I wasn't allowed to give the money away; I personally had to use it.

It surprised me that I didn't know what I wanted to

do, the only thing I felt I wanted to do was help people. I wanted the lives of others to be better. As I thought about the questions, soon I was saying I would open places of learning for Entrepreneurs. I would create business centers where people could come get advice on starting their own business. My additional thought was that I wanted to make this global, especially to the people of Brazil where I had lived in my early twenties. This answer was acceptable to them. I was starting to feel like I was passing their test.

We moved on to the next question. If I knew I only had ninety days left to live, what would I do? To my complete surprise, this question made me very emotional. For whatever reason tears came to my eyes. Here I was sitting in a home I had just decided to sell with two strangers crying. They sat there staring at me. Wow. I did not see that coming. They were both very kind and gracious. I pulled myself together; then commented to ease the tension in the room. My answers came to me, I would spend time with my family by taking them all on a vacation, I would be more dedicated to my religious practices and quiet my life to be closer to my God. I would also contact people in my life, family, friends and people I hadn't talked to in a long time and tell them I loved them. Silence fell over the room. I was trying to keep my composure. At the same time, thinking to myself, what are these men doing to me? This sucks, I'm not sure I like this.

They said okay great. We have what we need. They told me they would talk together to decide if I fit the profile of a person they would like to work with. They thanked me for my honesty and openness. They gave praise to my sweet Charlie and left. I turned and walked back up my stairs thinking that was really weird. They had asked me just two questions. One in which I answered very boldly with pride, and the other question made me cry. I thought to myself, they probably think I am a lunatic. At this point, it honestly didn't matter. I knew I was starting to understand the true inner workings of my heart. Not only did I understand my heart, I was also experiencing an additional amount of courage. I kept moving forward and that made me feel an immense amount of peace.

MY HOME

Within days of accepting the offer on my house, I sold the majority of my furniture and received an email from the idea management company. They had accepted me as a client. Wahoo! I was very happy. I didn't know where these decisions were going to take me but I felt an excitement I couldn't deny. I set up an appointment to start my program with the idea management company. The two men that came to meet me at my house were assigned to be my guides. I continued cleaning out my house and started looking for a new place to live.

The most important requirement for a new living space was that is was pet friendly. Charlie was moving with me. I looked at a few privately owned townhomes and apartments. They ended up not allowing pets so they wouldn't work. There was a place I wanted to check out about 10 minutes North of my home. I made an appointment with one of the leasing agents. The model apartment they showed me was small, like really small. I knew I committed to downsizing but that apartment did not feel right. The leasing agent mentioned there was an available one-bedroom apartment with a different floor plan. She asked if I wanted to take a look. I said, sure.

We walked to the opposite end of the apartment property. This apartment was bigger. It looked out east toward the mountains, which was nice. The thing I loved the most was that they would allow me to bring Charlie. I thanked the leasing agent. But, didn't make a decision that day. I wanted to make sure this was the right place.

Later, in the week I went to my first appointment with the idea management company. It was in a city west of Salt Lake City, Utah. I left early to ensure I would get there in time. The destination was at an office in the old United States Army depot. I had never been there. The depot felt extremely deserted. There were rows of empty silos covering acres of land. The place had an eerie feeling that made me nervous about what I was getting myself into.

Once I arrived and entered the building I knew I was safe. My assigned guides were waiting inside. They were both very kind as I remembered from the meeting at my house. They provided a happy and comfortable workspace. I was given a soft chair and comfortable blanket to wrap up in. Across from me there was a gigantic white board covering the wall. One guide sat at a desk; the other was in a chair similar to mine.

The first thing we did was talk about my answers to the questions they had asked me at my house. What I would do if I had five-billion dollars and what I would do if I only had 90-days to live. The answer I gave for the five-billion dollar question was that I wanted to help my family and take them all on a vacation with me. The second part was to give something back to the world. I wanted to do something of impact, something of worth. My guides started to ask me additional questions.

Why did I want to take my family on a vacation? Why was that something I would only be able to do if I had five-billion dollars? Why wasn't it something I could do now? I didn't know. I didn't have the money to pay for all of them to go on a vacation with me? But, why did I have to have money to vacation with them? There were ways to spend time together that were not expensive. Why in my mind was it connected to money?

These questions were thought provoking. I sat there thinking and searching. I presented a few ideas to my guides and they kept pushing me to go deeper. Eventually, it came out that I didn't feel like my family would want to spend time with me unless I forced them by paying for it. Kind of a crazy thought. I remembered from my first session with the energy healer that my six-year old self had been very sad and lonely. That might have been what was triggering me now. It may have been those feelings of loneliness that made me think I needed to buy a vacation for my family to spend time with me. My family was a good family. They were a great family.

I was the youngest of five siblings. We were all relatively close in age. All of my siblings had been married for decades, this made me feel very different from them. They all had kids and were done having kids and I hadn't even started. Admittedly this made me felt like an outsider. It made me feel like I hadn't accomplished as much as they had. It wasn't their fault. These were my own feelings, my own demons. They were exceptional people. My parents provided a safe and protected home. They had a loyal and loving relationship. All of my siblings included me in their lives. I was invited on vacations, to have sleepovers and to spend holidays lounging at their houses enjoying yummy food.

We switched to the 90-days to live question. My answer to the five-billion dollar question was that I wanted to pay to have my family spend time with me but my answer to the 90-days to live question was I wanted to spend time with my family and didn't care what we did, I just wanted us to be together. Those two things didn't match. With all the work I had done with the energy healer and the Keys to Confidence program there was still some unresolved issues I associated with my family. Any sadness or loneliness I still felt because of my family was on me. I wasn't because of them or the way they treated me.

The other answers to the 90-day question were to spend more time in worship of my God and to tell all the people in my life how much I loved them. These answers made me emotional. Tears rolled down my cheeks as I talked over them in more detail. I wanted the men in my past to know I forgave them for not treating me well and that I loved them. I also wanted other people I had let fizzle out of my life to know I loved them.

My guides said those were great things. They saw that they made me emotional. The next question they posed was why aren't you doing those things now? Why aren't you spending more time worshipping your God and telling people you love them? There was no reason.

I told my guides I wasn't doing that now because I wasn't going to die. One of the guides asked me, "How do you know you're not going to die? Have you been told how much time you have to live?" Wow. As simple as it was, I hadn't thought of that. He was right; I had no idea how much time I had to live. No one knows how much time they have to live.

My head was spinning. These guys were getting to some additional issues I was holding. It was tough to be this open with them. I felt extremely vulnerable. For the remainder of the meeting we talked about accountability and what that means in our lives.

I was given a homework assignment to study accountability. Especially personal accountability. They wanted to know what motivated me. They were going to determine this by having me define who I felt accountable to. I thought about the assignment as I drove home.

This was hard for me. I felt accountable to myself but I didn't know how to define it. Accountability with others was much easier to define. For example I felt accountable to my dog. He relied on my for his food and for all of his care. Just like a parent is accountable to a baby or child.

But how did I take care of myself? What values and morals did I hold myself personally accountable to? How did I stay true to those things? I had no idea. And for that night I was exhausted. I was home now and in my bed. I turned of the light and fell asleep.

sometimes you must SPEND TIME ALONE

GOALS are PERSONAL [9]

[9] To access printable artwork visit www.everysingledaycorporation.com

RELATIONSHIPS

Being days away from closing on my house I needed to decide where I wanted to live. I went back to the apartment complex that I liked and asked to see the second apartment again. This time the leasing agent gave me the key and let me go to the apartment myself.

I walked across the property to the end of the buildings to the vacant apartment. I opened the door. This time I walked around slowly asking myself, "Is this going to be my new home?" I stood on the balcony looking in the direction of the mountains. I got sidetracked for a minute staring at the majesty of the mountains. I started thinking about the mountains strength, their form, their grandeur. They were immovable. They knew their place in the world and they held that space confidently, boldly and unapologetically. There were very few things that existed that could destroy them. I walked back into the apartment. It was cute, quaint, and simple. It was going to work.

I carefully locked the door and walked back to the leasing office. I asked a few clarifying questions and told them I wanted to rent the apartment. I was doing this. Ahhhh! I felt a little crazy. I hadn't lived in an apartment in 11 years. It was going to be fine. There were some things that were very exciting about living in an apartment The top things on my list, the pool, not having to deal with snow removal or taking care of a yard.

I left the complex with the necessary paperwork. Everything was coming together nicely. I felt very happy! Good things were happening and I was feeling free. As I drove back home I felt an intense sense of calm come over me. I knew I was on the right path.

As I was cleaning out the rooms in my home and preparing to move I was surprised how easy it was for me to process the thought of moving. I was very fond of the memories I made in this home. I hosted family parties, numerous niece and nephew sleepovers, birthdays, missionary farewell parties, and dinners, New Year's Eve parties, neighborhood gatherings, a wedding, baby showers, wedding showers, yard sales, and world cup soccer parties. I also received my master's degree in this home and started my catering business.

This home represented a big portion of my life and my identity. There were a lot of memories, I was boxing up and leaving. It was a therapeutic experience to be thinking about these things while preparing to move on.

In the midst of packing up my life I had another appointment scheduled with my guides. At this meeting we were going to review accountability and define some relationships in my life. They had a list of eight relationship categories they wanted to go over with me.

The list started with a higher power; human beings with sub categories of family, friends and fellow men; animals; environment; inanimate objects and myself. The plan was to review all of these relationships and put them in order of importance on the gigantic white board on the wall.

This felt like a daunting task. We started with my "higher power". What did this mean to me? For some, this is God, an all knowing being who created the heavens and the earth, for others, it might be a saint, or scientific philosophy. To some, it is a term they call the Universe or another pattern of thought. For others, it might be an object or item. The possibilities are endless for what a higher power could be. For me, it was God, the creator, my Heavenly Father. The title I personally have for him is Pai Celestial. The Portuguese title for Heavenly Father I adopted while living in Brazil in my early twenties. Most of the time I just lovingly called him Pai.

The next relationship we tackled was "myself". There were a few things that were easy for me to define. I knew I was good at being a boss. I was good at organizing and running businesses. I also knew there was a quiet young girl inside of me named Annie. She was the one who had been working so hard to protect me for so long. We put the titles of the boss and Annie went on the white. There was another part of me that loved food. I called her Fat Annie. She helped control my emotions through eating, and making sure I always felt full. There was a part of me that loved service; another part was a leader, There was also a fun and happy side of me I called fun-loving Laurann. My spirit, the being of creation that came to this earth to live in a mortal body was the last. She was the person I knew the least about at this point in my life. I knew she was inside of me but I didn't always hear her voice. Her name was appropriately, Laurann.

I was defined. All of the different parts of staring me in the face from a gigantic white board. The boss, Annie, fat Annie, the leader, the servant, fun-loving Laurann, and my beautifully created spirit Laurann.

YOUR RELATIONSHIP WITH
• YOURSELF •
sets the tone
FOR EVERY OTHER
RELATIONSHIP
• YOU HAVE •

[10]

We defined all of the other relationship in my life that night as well. My "family" consisted of being a daughter, a sister and an aunt. We included future wife and mother under family as well. My "friend" lists consisted of

---

[10] To access printable artwork visit www.everysingledaycorporation.com

childhood friends, best friends I spent most of my time with, and one on one friends that had great importance in my life. My "fellowmen" were people I went to church with or others that I met in the general public.

The "animal" category to me was Charlie. My dear sweet Charlie boy. "Inanimate objects" included my catering company and my new apartment. The aspects of the "environment" that meant the most to me were the ocean and the mountains. They way I defined all of these things was by naming the things that were the most important to me or the things for which I felt the most pride.

There was my list. It took hours and hours to put all of this together. During my next meeting we placed all of these relationships in order of importance in my life. To be able to do this my guides asked a undeterminable number of comparison questions. Meaning they would take two different defined relationships in my life and compare them to one another to see which one came out as the more important one in my life. Questions like if you had to choose between going on a once in a lifetime beach vacation with your friends or a once in a life time opportunity to go spend a week with your family in a beautiful mountain cabin what would you choose?

There were some scenarios that were easy to decide others took 20 – 30 minutes to talk through to help me make up my mind. All of this was very intense. There were a few times when I felt extreme anger. And more than one time I told my guides I didn't like them.

I really wanted to give the right answers. In my mind there was a certain way my list of relationships should look. My family for sure should be first. My higher power should be number one as well, but then what about me? Where was my position in the list? Examining each of these relationships was one of the most eye-opening experiences I had ever had in my life! I had never thought about the importance of knowing where each of these relationships fell in my life.

And after a couple of hours, a million deep breaths, a fair amount of heartache, and some free falling tears we were finished. My list of relationships in order of importance was complete. My family came first, my parents, siblings, nieces and nephews, along with my future spouse and children. My dear sweet Charlie boy was second on the list. Then came my friends, my higher power and myself. After my higher power came my fellow men, the environment and inanimate objects. My guides asked me to stand by the wall sized white board and we took a picture to document all of the work I had completed.

TRUE OR FALSE

A few days after this last meeting with my guides I went to my parent's house to stay for the weekend. The day for me to close on my house was fast approaching. I was working in the basement kitchen in my parent's house making some waffles when my realtor called.

There was a problem with selling my house. The buyer for my house didn't get approved for financing. That meant the people we accepted the offer from couldn't purchase the house. I didn't know how did that happened. I thought they had a pre-approval letter. My relator told me they did have a pre-approval letter but apparently there were some problems with a tax return.

I had just signed the lease on my new apartment. Which in the past would have made me panic. But, I felt completely calm about having the sale of my house fall through. I knew I was supposed to be moving so I didn't worry about it. My relator put my house back on the market. We received a few requests for showings right away. For whatever reason, I was prompted to let my neighbor know my house was back on the market. She had mentioned knowing an interested buyer the first time it was on the market. She said that the person she knew was interested. I sent her the name and phone number of my realtor. Within ninety minutes my relator called me back and let me know my house had been sold, again. My neighbor's contact wanted to buy it. This time we didn't need to wait for financing. The offer was a full market value cash offer.

I finished cleaning out my home and packing up my things. I sold almost all of my furniture and belongings. I was keeping my bed and a few other pieces of furniture. I came to the realization that these things were just things. They in no way, shape or form defined who I was. My value and worth were inside of me. My worth was my soul. The spirit that lived in my human body.

I started putting together my new living space. It very quickly became my home. I was excited to be moving into a smaller, cozier, personal space. I felt good about my life. I had feelings of joy that were flooding over me.

The day for me to close on my house came. I was so excited. My new apartment was all set up and Charlie and I had moved. I was ready. It was a Tuesday morning. It was the day of the 2016 presidential election. I had sent in my voter card early so I decided I wanted to spend the morning in religious worship. I went to a local LDS temple that was close to the home I sold.

It was a peaceful morning. I felt contentment. My heart felt open and full. When I was finished with my worship service. I walked out to the parking lot to get into my car. I only had a few hours before the appointment to sign the papers on my house. I started my car and began to back out of the parking spot. Suddenly my car stopped and wouldn't move. I couldn't turn the steering wheel. It was stuck. My heart sank a little bit. I pushed on the brakes. I was now sitting half in the parking spot and half way out. I looked to see if any other cars were coming. There were none.

I was stumped. Maybe my car just needed to be restarted. I turned off the ignition and took the key out. I put the key back in the ignition and turned on my car. It started. I put it in drive and tried pull forward. I couldn't turn the steering wheel. There was a definitely a problem. I used all my might to turn the wheel enough to get my car back into the parking spot. I sat there not knowing exactly what to do. I quickly saw a few scenarios come to my mind. First, I needed to call the car dealership. I just had the power-steering pump replaced a few months before. That was likely the issue.

From there, I would just have to figure out how to get my car to the dealership and then find a ride down to the appointment to sign the papers on my house. I called the car dealership. They agreed that it was likely the power-steering pump, They apologized that I had any issues. It really wasn't their fault. Stuff happens. Sometimes cars wear out or power-steering pumps break. I didn't believe anyone had maliciously tried to sabotage my day. They gave me the phone number of a car towing company. They would pay to have my car towed and for the repairs.

I called the car towing company. The gentleman that answered the phone also apologized for me having such a bad day. I laughed a little. I wasn't having a bad day. It was fine. The power-steering pump was out in my car that was all. I was in a parking lot. I wasn't driving down the road or on a hill. No harm was caused. I was fine. Honestly, I felt protected, the situation of losing my power-steering could have been a million times worse.

The car was taken care of, now I just needed to get down to the closing appointment for my house. Three options popped into my mind, I could call an Uber driver, or my friend who was on maternity leave with her baby or I could call my realtor. He was going to the same place I was and his office was about two miles away from where I currently was. I called him first.

He answered and asked if I was ready for the day. I told him I most certainly was but that I had one small problem and I needed his help. He agreed that he could come pick me up. We laughed about it a little. He needed to run a few errands. We grabbed a quick lunch and went over to the title company to sign the papers.

The agent at the title company was very kind. My realtor knew her well so we talked about a variety of things unrelated to selling homes. We laughed and became comfortable with each other. I signed all of the papers. My home was sold. It was no longer mine and longer something I used to define my worth. My relator and I left the title company office. He drove me to the car dealership to pick up my car. It was fixed and ready. Everything worked out just fine.

I was settled into my cozy little apartment. And I had stepped away from another job that wasn't fulfilling me. Financially I made enough money from selling my home I wouldn't have to work for a while. I didn't have any debt or a car payment. My financial responsibilities had also dramatically changed now that I moved into an apartment. I didn't have to pay for all the expenses of owning a home. I was free to do whatever I wanted. I saw friends for lunch; I went to matinee movies with my parents. I read books, I went to the gym, I walked Charlie, and I took long middle of the day bubble baths. I took naps, I had Netflix binge days, and I took a trip to see my sister who lived in Oregon.

Life was awesome. I was very happy to be free of chains that had been holding me back. Most of all the chain of feeling like I was making everyone else happy while I was miserable. The hardest thing for me during this time of newfound freedom in my life was that, eventually I knew I would need to go back to work. I could live for a while without working, but I was thirty-seven now. I wasn't ready to be all the way done working yet.

Another thing that started nagging me was that I loved being productive. I liked completing tasks. I found value in a hard day's work. Now my value was connected to me and just me. In the last several months I had gone from being an executive in a company to working in the finance industry to selling my home and almost everything I had to living in an apartment with no job. Sometimes it was a lot to process.

One day while I was sitting at the counter of my apartment thinking about all of the changes I made. I felt a great need to review the relationship list I had recently put together at the idea management company. Something on that list was bothering. I pulled out the notes I had taken during the meetings. I knew I could figure this out. Through the healing work and other meditation moments my mind had learned to be a great navigator of issues and how to reason through what was truth.

I wanted to review what the placement of each relationship on my list meant. Any relationship that was above me on the list set the terms for that relationship. Meaning if, my friends and family were on the list above me they set the terms for our relationship. They set all the expectations, they dictate what I will and will not do. They are the keepers of what choices I make about my life. They were higher on my list than I was which meant they were more important to me than I was to me.

I looked at my list and saw that I had placed myself fourth on my list and the placement of God, my Higher Power, Pai Celestial, was fifth. My family was first, Charlie was second, and my friends were third. I was saying my family, friends and Charlie set the terms for my life and I was going to set the terms for God in my life. Immediately I knew my list was not in the order of how I truly felt and wasn't what I wanted.

Another thing was that, when talking about animals, it included ALL animals, not just my handsome, perfect, rescue dog, Charlie. I spent some time reworking my list. I knew there were some things that were out of place. I talked with Heavenly Father about my list. I talked with him about my relationships. I also examined the feelings I had about myself. Did I want myself to be in charge of my life? If I did, I needed to move myself on my relationship list much closer to the top.

I pondered these things for a while. I read over the notes I had from the meetings. I prayed, I meditated, I cried. I really wanted to love myself. I wanted to be able to look at myself in the eyes and know without question I had value.

I also didn't want to set the terms for God in my life. That was crazy. He is God. I didn't know better than He did. He already knew the path of my life. As I spent the quiet time to reformulate and design my list, it naturally all started flowing into my mind. My Higher Power, Pai Celestial was first. He was my creator, my father, and my biggest fan. If anyone wanted me to have success, it was him. Second on my list was myself. All the different parts of me. The list continued with, my family, my friends, animals, inanimate objects and the environment. I ran my hand over the new list I had written and then I sat and cried. I felt reassurance that the new list was my truth.

It is hard for me to find the words to explain what I felt as I realized the most important relationship in my life was my relationship with my God. The second most important relationship I had was with myself. By writing those words down in a list and accepting them I was declaring that the only people setting terms in my life were my God and myself, and that was extremely empowering.

I had another meeting set up with my guides. It was time to get deeper into who I was. They had done some research on me. They looked through my Facebook profile. Initially I was a little scared when I heard they had cyber stalked me. What did they find? I had set up a business page when I worked at the financial company. They pulled my profile description from there.

The description listed my degrees, my work experience, the major events I had accomplished in my life. I talked about the ownership I had in the companies I started. As they were reading the profile to me, I said, "Yes, that's me." I'd done quite a bit with my life. I felt very proud. One of them then said to me, "So, who really is Laurann?" I felt a little confused. He had just read an entire page on who I was. I grew up in a small town, lived in a foreign country, had a bachelor's degree, a master's degree, and was a Vice President at a company. Owned my own company, he had all the relevant information. What did he mean?

He explained what he meant, "These are all really awesome things that you have done with your life. You have an impressive resume. You list accomplishments of your life and job titles. But, that's what they are, job titles and college degrees. They tell me nothing about who you are."

He invited me step up to the white board. He asked me to make two columns. At the top of one of the columns I wrote "true" at the top of the other column I wrote "false".

Then he proceeded to ask me, "While you were growing up on the small farm in Northern Utah what did you learn?" That was an easy one. I learned to work hard and how to be a member of a team. Okay great, I wrote hard worker under the title of "true". We moved on to the next thing. "What did you learn while you were living in a foreign country?" This one was also easy, independence and how to be resourceful. Awesome. I added those things to the list under "true". We went through every last detail of my Facebook profile list. Being a Vice President made me a leader. Receiving my Master's Degree taught me to be dedicated. Opening my own company helped me learn to be forward thinking and organized.

As I sat there looking at my list of truths I was proud. That was who I was, Laurann. I was a dedicated, resourceful, forward thinking, organized leader who loved education and was a member of a family, who knew she was a daughter of God! That was me.

The side of the board with the word "false" showed my list of accomplishments such as my college degrees, the company I had started and my job titles. Those things helped form and are a part of who I have become.

Unveiling all of these "truths" and "fallacies" helped me realized I didn't need to compete with anyone else. I am able to be proud of who I am. I gained a greater

---

[11] To access printable artwork visit www.everysingledaycorporation.com

understanding of who I was. The work I put in to earning my degrees and my career are very important to me. At times in my life it is appropriate for me to list them and speak of the amazing accomplishments.

Because of the unique personal experiences in my life no one else could be me and I couldn't be anyone else. There is absolutely only one version of each of us. No amount of trying, competition or comparison will ever, ever, ever, make two people completely alike.

HE NEEDS ME

A few months after I had sold my house I realized I was bored. I was bored out of my mind. I was used to working and keeping myself so busy I rarely had time to sit and think. Now all I did was think. I knew I was not supposed to be working. But I was questioning if it really was okay for me to just be taking baths and watching Netflix.

I found myself making an appointment to go see the energy healer again. I sat down with her, and I explained that, I was going crazy. I had carried out the changes I felt inspired to make but what was next? Surely there was something more for me to be doing. She smiled because she could feel that the energy I was carrying demonstrated that I was on purpose. I didn't need to be doing anything else at the moment. My mind and body needed time to relax, sit and be at peace. My energy was shifting from masculine to feminine.

I spent so many years being wound up looking for my next project, beating deadlines, pushing myself, growing, learning, and trying to force things to happen. I had mostly lived in masculine energy. Female energy is a softer, gentler energy. Masculine energy is more robust and tough. It wasn't a bad thing to live in masculine energy but it didn't leave much time for relaxation in my life. For me to have complete balance and happiness I need to be equal in both. Others may have a different formula that keeps them happy. I just knew this was mine.

I was shifting into a more feminine mindset. She started to explain the aspects of feminine energy using the example of a spider. Wait. I had been told about spiders before. My friend Nancy, the author of the Keys to Confidence program, had told me a spider could bring things into our lives. The healer affirmed this belief. Spiders have feminine energy. They are creators of beautiful elaborate webs. They use their webs to attract things. They don't go out hunting. They attract. They sit and wait perched up perfectly in their web until what they want comes to them. I loved it. I swore I would never squish another spider again.

As I was talking with the energy healer something else came up in our discussion. It was something I still believed about myself. It had come up in my meeting with the guides from the idea management company. I felt I wasn't good enough. There was a bit of unknowing in my mind of my true value. We talked and cleared out some beliefs I was feeling. Things like I wasn't smart enough or I wasn't into popular trends like others. At times, I felt very inadequate. To replace my feelings of inadequacy I worked to find a word that was the opposite of inadequate. I meditated with the energy healer and the word that came to mind was cherished. That was it, I wanted to be cherished. We walked through a mediation method to allow the concept of being cherished to settle into my heart.

Later that night I attended a class about knowing how to have safe, energetic boundaries around family during the holidays. The class was meant to teach you how to not get in a fight over mashed potatoes. There were a lot of great messages shared. One of the presenters passed around sheets of paper and pencils. She wanted us to write down things we had been struggling with. For me, my relationship list came to my mind. I was feeling ashamed that I hadn't put my Higher Power at the top of my list during my first try. I knew it was time for me to meditate and let go of guilt I felt because of this.

I took time during this class to silently talk to my Pai Celestial. I humbly expressed my sorrow to Him that I hadn't been as connected to Him as I needed to be. I apologized that I had let the pressures of the world; society and success become my driving force. As I sat there talking with Pai, a distinct message came to mind, that it was okay. He knew I was learning. He loved me and He needed me to help Him with His plan. I had never thought of that. It may sound crazy but I thought, He is God, He can do whatever He wants. He created the world, made the sea and the sun and the stars. He didn't need me. He was God. He is the almighty creator. Why would He need a girl like me? In that moment I knew, He did indeed need me. The truth is, that He needs all us. He isn't mortal; He doesn't live here with us. He needs us to learn to love ourselves and pass that love onto others. To help each other fulfill our true destinies on earth.

I DIDN'T KNOW YOU NEEDED me

Of course, like so many other moments I had over the past few months, I began to cry. My body was covered in goose bumps. I knew I was loved, honored, cherished, wanted and needed by my Pai Celestial. All of the changes I was prompted to make, leaving my job and selling my house were putting me in a place to be able serve others and help them find their own way, and to shine their own light. These moments of connection with my Higher Power filled my heart with immense joy and made me extremely happy.

The following day I was meeting with my guides at

---

[12] To access printable artwork visit www.everysingledaycorporation.com

the idea management company for another appointment. They had studied our previous sessions and found an answer to the core motivator of my life. I headed to the appointment with plenty of time and arrived a little early. I sat in my car and to let my heart and mind be quiet.

As we started the meeting, I was excited for the big reveal. What was my motivation for doing anything? Was it money, prestige or power? Those were options I knew motivated people. Through months we had been meeting they were looking for trends. They told me there was one main concept that kept coming up. They said that out of all the data they had analyzed and collected the best way to describe my motivator in life was to be cherished.

I was a bit confused. I had just met with the energy healer the day before and she had told me I wanted to be cherished. I asked my guides if they had talked to her. They said that they hadn't. I explained that I had just met with her yesterday. I had been talking about how hard it has been for me to just sit still in my life and that I felt inadequate. She helped me discover that all I wanted was to be cherished. They laughed and said, "that's really cool".

The energy healer worked with matters involving the heart. My guides worked with logic involving the brain. During the last several months, since walking away from my job as a company executive to taking naps and walking my dog my heart and mind had been working to become one and it finally happened. They were in sync. All I truly wanted in my life was to be cherished.

MONEY

I continued enjoying my non-work, no responsibilities life.
I spent time with my family and friends during the
holidays. Not worrying about working in between parties
and events was such a nice situation to enjoy. I was truly
spoiled. After my trip to Oregon to see my sister, I took a
trip to Disneyland with some friends. While I was in
Disneyland I got the news that one of my nephews, was
engaged. He had met a nice young girl a couple of months
before and they decided they wanted to get married.

I love all of my nieces and nephews dearly. When I
heard this news it hurt my heart. Not because of my
nephew or because of the darling girl he was going to
marry but because I felt I shined a light on the fact that I
still wasn't married.

The feelings that rushed into my heart and mind were
not happy. It made me sad. It took me to that old place of

shame, anger and frustration, a place of questioning why hadn't I met someone I wanted to marry. All I wanted my entire adult life was to be married.

These feelings forced me to turn to the new truths I learned. What was the trigger that brought this sadness? I thought about love, and its importance in our lives. I pondered the institution of marriage and exactly what it meant. I thought of the expectations society has for people to get married. I asked Pai Celestial to help me understand and honor the feelings I was having about my nephew's engagement.

Powerful instructive thoughts entered my mind. An understanding of the concept of age and time came to me. Age and time are only relevant in our mortal minds. If we think outside our mortal existence it did not matter who got married first or last. You could be eighteen or eighty-eight and the blessings you receive from marriage would be the same.

In addition the fact that my nephew was getting married before me had absolutely no bearing on whether my life was a success. I had just spent months learning that my success doesn't have the tiniest thing to do with others or their choices.

The next thing that came to my mind was that, my marriage, when it came into my life, was going to be a crowning blessing in my life. Lastly, love was love and I love love. Young love, old love, singular love, family love, it was all from the same unbiased source. Feeling sad or bitter for my nephew's happiness was only going to hurt me. He was going to get married and move forward with his life and not give me a second thought. I could accept it and support it or I could be mad and waste my energy on something that had little impact in my life.

I remember the time I sat with the energy healer and discussed marriage. Marriage does not guarantee happiness, connection, devotion, love or stability. Things we accomplish in life don't give us a free pass to all of life's blissful pleasures. Marriage is just something that happens. Knowing who you are, looking yourself in the eyes and knowing your own majesty and worth. That is what makes you a complete person.

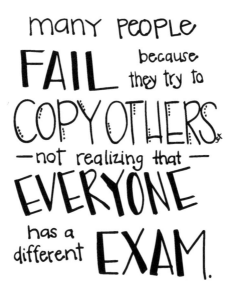

13

After the holidays passed I met with my guides a few more times. I started listing the things I wanted to do with my life. Business ideas I had. The list became a several pages long. We studied the five-billion dollar question and

---

[13] To access printable artwork visit www.everysingledaycorporation.com

the 90-days to live question again. I wrote down all my ideas. There were a lot!

Ideas on my list included working at Barnes and Noble, applying to be a Business Professor, opening a bakery, teaching a cooking class, writing a cookbook, opening a business consulting business, being a home organizer, being a home decorator, being a real estate home stager, being a personal shopper, opening a bed and breakfast, being a fitness instructor, opening a restaurant for my catering business, opening a commercial kitchen, opening a lounge, doing hand lettering and art projects, on and on and on. While I was making the list, I went back and studied old journal entries. In the journal, I had used in the Keys to Confidence program I had written down that I believed I would reach great potential. I also wrote that I wanted to be a pillar of light and at times I allowed others to hold me back. I honestly had a desire to help and lift others.

In another journal I wrote that I wanted to create a place of comfort. I wanted to share the light and authenticity I found for myself to inspire and encourage others to do the same. I wanted to show, share and have everyone feel love. I wanted to expand people's perceptions and understanding. I wanted to allow them the opportunity to release things in their life they were holding onto that weren't necessary. I wanted individuals to stand boldly in their own confidence, strongly in their beliefs without apology.

Now that I had my list of options, and knowing my life motivator was to be cherished, my work with the idea management company was finished. I felt it was time for me to get back to working. I reviewed the items on my list of business ideas and decided I wanted to open a commercial kitchen. The kitchen was going to be a place for people to gather to learn different cooking techniques. It was going to be a space I would rent out for events and parties. It was going to be beautiful.

I made a list of what I needed to accomplish this new goal. As I did, a few obstacles came to my mind. I needed money. I hadn't worked in few months. I had enough money to live on but I needed money to build a kitchen, furnish it, and hire employees to help me.

I meditated and talked with Pai Celestial. I expressed to him that I needed money to come into my life. I didn't know how this is going to happen but I knew that he could provide a way for it to happen. I believed that it would come.

I didn't have a script I just said the truths that came to my heart with all of my mind and soul and power. I had set intentions before. In the summer I asked for financial clients to come into my life and to meet a man. Those things had come. But they didn't stay in my life. I was in a much different mind space now then I had been in before. I knew the power of the relationship I had with my Higher Power and I knew the intents of my heart were completely pure.

I left that intention for money to come into my life and didn't concentrate on it too much. As I was working on my goals toward opening my kitchen an unsettled matter in my life kept coming to my mind. When I left my job as an executive in health care industry I was angry. I was really upset with the owners of that business. I felt abandoned and undervalued by them and it caused me to have a lot of anger. The feeling I was getting was that I needed to reconcile with them and completely let go of the bad feelings I had towards them.

Along with that, another person came to my mind that I needed to reconcile with. It was my old coworker from the financial company. We had been friends and then while we worked together things happened that affected our friendship. It weighed on my mind. I knew I needed to reach out to all of these people before I could move forward.

I didn't feel right about just texting them or calling them up. It had been a long time since I talked to any of them. Again, I decided to talk to my higher power about my intentions to reconcile. I whole heartedly asked him to provide a way for me to reconcile. I left it at that.

A day or so later, I took Charlie out for a walk. He always went to the same exact bush in the same exact flowerbed to pee. I was looking at the ground waiting for him to finish and there was a quarter lying in the dirt. I looked at it and smiled. It was money! It was only a quarter but money had come into my life. I picked it up, I was so happy. I wanted to keep it. I wanted it to be evidence of my intention of money coming into my life. I found a special jar in my house and I put my quarter in it. I named it my money intention jar. [14]

The next day I took Charlie out for a walk we went down the path a little farther. I looked down and there was another quarter. This time I laughed. Two days in a row now while walking Charlie, I found a quarter. The next day, while I was out with Charlie again, there was another quarter. Three days and three quarters. It was not

---

[14] For more about understanding your relationship with money visit www.everysingledaycorporation.com

a coincidence. I put all of them in my money jar. The next day I found a dime in the rocks. The day after that I looked down and saw a penny. Day after day I was receiving manifestations of money. I was honoring every last penny I saw. I was finding money on a daily basis it was amazing. All of the money went into my jar.

Then other things started happening that brought different forms of money into my life. I went to my parent's house for dinner and my mom pulled out a fifty-dollar gift card. She said she wasn't going to use it, so she gave it to me. That was free money. The next week I got a check in the mail from my sister. I forgot she was going to send it. It was more money. The other thing that started happening was people started to offer me things for free or to do things for me for free that I generally paid for. All of this was money. Saved money or found. I was honoring the power of my intention and being rewarded for it.

When I set my intention for money, I didn't set any limits with it. I didn't ask for a specific amount or try to determine the way in which it would come. I said, I wanted it to come, and I released it. The ability of creation was awakening inside of me. A few weeks later I found eleven dollars in the hallway at the movie theatre. Who finds money at the movie theatre? To this day the list of ways money comes into my life continues.

All of the abundance that was coming to me was because I had done the work to release my old stubborn mindset and worked daily to be connected to my higher power. I loved the new amazing life he was helping me to create.

INTENTIONS

I became very accustomed to practicing meditation in my life. I would play music or lay quietly in my bed and listen to the sound of my breathing while I allowed my mind to wander. One afternoon after going to the gym, I was mediating in bed and the doorbell rang. Usually it was a delivery guy bringing me a package from Amazon.

I went to the door in my leggings, t-shirt and messed up mediation hair. It wasn't the Amazon delivery guy. There were two men standing on my apartment doorstep from the FBI. That wasn't what I expected. I turned to one of them and recognized him immediately. He had been one of the agents that came to the health care company office. The other gentlemen looked familiar as well. I asked if I knew him from somewhere. He confirmed that he had been to the office as well. I had seen both of these men before. They asked me if we could talk for a few minutes.

When I left my employment at the health care company there was an ongoing undetermined government inquiry. I knew from having dealt with the government agencies before that I had the right not to speak to them. I told them I had legal representation and that I wouldn't talk to them without my lawyer. They knew I knew my rights. They handed me a letter and I closed my door. The exact moment the door closed I realized this was my answer.

This was the way I was going to reach out to my old bosses to reconcile with them for having left their place of work feeling nasty. That may seem unusual to some but for me it was the answer. I had specifically asked for an opportunity to reach out to them. In that moment I knew the answer had come.

I walked around my apartment feeling stunned. My prayers, my thoughts and intentions were being answered. I was becoming a master of understanding what I needed and how to attain it. I sent both of my old bosses a text. We got on the phone. I had the opportunity to offer an apology and grant my forgiveness for the feelings I had. We had a pleasant conversation and they both hoped I was doing well.

I really couldn't believe all that was happening. Money was coming into my life and I had been given a way to reconcile with my old employers. There were many things in my life to be happy about.

I had a hair appointment scheduled with my friend and stylist the following day. I was telling her all of these stories about my intentions finally working. She was astonished at how I had learned to attract things into my life. I felt inspired, she felt inspired. Life was very exciting.

After my hair appointment, we decided to grab a quick lunch together.

As I stepped into the restaurant the person sitting at the first table inside of the door was my former co-worker from the financial company. There she was. My other intention of reconciliation was being fulfilled. At this point I started to feel like I was living in an alternate universe.

She noticed me and I walked over to the table. I told her I had been thinking of her and was happy to be able to see her. She stood and we hugged. I didn't need to talk to her about what had happened. I knew when we embraced all had been forgiven by both sides. I could feel it in my heart. She looked good and happy and was working. That was all I wanted. I told her again that she had been on my mind and that I hoped her life was going well and that she had all the things she needed and wanted. It was a quick interaction but it was enough.

All of my intentions came to me. I could not deny that I had a God. That He was good and that He cared about what was happening in my life. I knew I had light and power inside of me. My life was becoming more. I no longer had a feeling of emptiness and wanting inside of me. My own light, the light inside of me was my power. I could be a learn and do anything I wanted to do. The choice was mine.

I started telling people I was going to open a commercial kitchen to teach classes and create a space for people to come for special events. All the people I shared the idea with loved it. They thought it was a cool business platform. I drove around looking for a location. I went to a few kitchen appliance wholesalers to get ideas on what type of equipment I wanted. I came up with a name for the kitchen and had a logo made. I was going to call it Forever Cherished. I wanted it to remind me of my motivator to be cherished.

As I was going through this process and working on a business plan and meditating, things were not coming together quite as I had expected. I kept hitting mind blocks. I couldn't figure out a location. I looked at lots of options. I couldn't decide exactly how I was going to make the venture profitable. I started to realizing that maybe this wasn't the right thing for me to be pursuing.

As I thought about what I wanted my work life to look like, I made a list of three things I wanted. I wanted to keep my free schedule, I wanted to do something that provided a good source of income and I wanted to feel like the work I was doing was providing value.

Around this same time, I was introduced to a book called, "The Universe Has Your Back" by Gabrielle Bernstein.[15] I downloaded the audio version and immediately started listening. This book has tremendous lessons in it. Usually when I am listening to an audio book I am working out, cleaning or have it on in the background. While listening to this book I sat with a journal writing and processing the message. It was the perfect book to solidify all the work I had been doing to overcome my fears.

I learned immense lessons on trusting that a great plan existed for me. In the book she uses The Universe as a higher power. I believe that God and The Universe have the same power. My beliefs are that God created The Universe so the power of The Universe is God's power.

---

[15] To read my full review of "The Universe Has Your Back" and other recommended books visit www.everysingledaycorporation.com

They will always create a greater outcome in our lives than we can if we let go and trust that they will do what they promise.

During this time, a few different companies approached me to work with them as a business consultant. One hired me as a business executor. That meant I was the person in the business that got things done. Another business wanted me to go through their program and provide feedback. As I started working with these companies, I realized I was coming upon my one-year anniversary of leaving my job in the health care industry.

I felt like a completely different person than the girl who sat on the floor crying in her home office looking at the box of contents she brought home after quitting her job. I was strong and confident. I knew my worth and value didn't depend on the responses, competition or comparison of others. I was me and that was more than good enough. I loved me, all the different parts of me.

The suggestion was made to me by a good friend that I take one week in the next month to celebrate and honor the healing I had been through. To celebrate all of the change I had embraced in the last year. I canceled all the plans I had for the following week so I could spend the week honoring myself.

The first thing I did during this week was go to a local restaurant during the dinner hour and sit down at a table by myself. I felt extremely uncomfortable. I had done it many times before when I traveled for work. But this was different, people I knew might see me. It didn't matter though because I knew I was doing it for me and I wasn't responsible for their judgments.

The dinner was very pleasant. I had a very nice conversation with the waiter and the hostess of the restaurant. They were both very kind and might I say nicer to me because I was alone. I loved the experience. It was so nice to sit down and enjoy a meal by myself feeling absolutely happy with who I was.

Next, there was a movie I wanted to see. I ended up getting to the movie late. The theatre didn't have assigned seats and it was packed. There was only one seat left in between two families. A single seat in the middle of the row. Awesome, I scooted right in there to that middle seat. In between those two families.

I loved being at the movie alone. Sitting there by myself doing nothing but enjoying it. I didn't feel any type of insecurity or reason to justify why I was there alone. The week I was spending with myself was intoxicating.

I spent time getting a manicure and pedicure. I also cleaned out my closet and bought some new clothes. I figured new clothes were a great way to celebrate the changed person I had become. I bought clothes that made me feel feminine and beautiful. Clothes that may not have been a part of the latest trends but they were clothes that were authentic to me and I loved them.

The best activity I had planned for the week was when I took myself to see The Lion King musical. I got dressed in one of my favorite new dresses. Took myself out to another dinner and went to the theatre.

I felt so much love in my heart for the love I was showing myself. Nothing I had experienced in my life felt better. I was ultimately proving to myself that I was important; I was allowing myself to be the most bright, authentic, person I could be. Not one thing or person in that moment was going to be able to stop me. They couldn't. I wasn't answering to them. I was answering to myself. I was honoring my own mind, my own body and my own spirit. I felt AMAZING!

The Lion King musical was one of the best musicals I had ever seen. I made friends with the people sitting on both sides of me. They asked me if I was there with someone. I very proudly and confidently said "No, I'm here alone." They all thought it was so cool. They commented on how incredible it was that I had brought myself to a musical. They also mentioned they didn't feel they were brave enough to do it. I encouraged them that they absolutely were brave enough. There was no reason they couldn't do it if I could do it. Anyone could do it if they choose to do so. I was no braver than anyone else. I had just given myself permission to not only face my fears but to conquer them.

My heart truly changed. I no longer thought that marriage was going to solve my problems. The desire to get married hadn't changed but I wasn't dwelling on it. I still look forward to meeting the man that was in my dreams. I think of him often and fantasize about our wonderful life together. My worth was no longer associated with whether I was married or not or the kind of job I had or the house I owned. My value was me. Me as a beautiful, bright and courageous woman.

I drove home that night completely and utterly satisfied with the week I had spent honoring myself. Someone else who might choose to do a similar experiment would likely do things different than what I had done. They would do things that would honor them in the best way possible.

I was proud to be who I was. I was excited about where my life had led me. I was happy with the training I had received through different experiences in my life. I understood in those moments as I drove home that I could be absolutely me in any and every circumstance I faced in my life. My own light was my power.

A few weeks later as I was driving to meet a friend. I understood that opening a commercial kitchen wasn't my course of life. It wasn't my true destiny. The mental blocks I was hitting wouldn't leave me. They were the reason I knew the kitchen wasn't the right path for me. There was a bud of something bigger inside of me. I had been avoiding it. I had been scared to embrace what was calling to me.

I had known for a few months and had glimpses of it in earlier years in my life. I knew what my Higher Power needed. He had pointed it out to me over and over again through my experiences. He wanted me to stand up boldly as a light to those who felt hurt or felt like they were in darkness. He wanted me to help lift those who stumbled. He wanted me to show them their own true path and way. He wanted me to inspire and encourage others.

Then I realized, I wanted me to help show people their true path. I wanted me to help lift those that stumbled. I wanted to inspire and encourage others. I knew this was my soul purpose. It was my desire as well as the desire of my Higher Power. It was my core story. Going through the process of cherishing myself and loving myself brought me to the place of understanding I was going to be able to help others.

My light was going to shine so that they could join me and shine their own light. Their own light would be their power. I uttered in a firm unwavering voice as I drove down the freeway, "I accept".

When I got home I sat down. I pulled out my computer I opened up a blank file and started typing. I was going to write my book the book I had thought about for years. A book that I titled *Every Single Day* with the subtitle *Your Own Light Is Your Power.*

EPILOGUE

I have sat here for the last few weeks of my life writing these thoughts and experiences in this book. I have cried, I laughed and I smiled. I have stopped to think and process. I've taken journeys back in time in the course of the last year and come up with an intense, powerful feeling of gratitude. There were so many things that came into and blessed my life in the past twelve months. The absolute only reason, they happened was because I allowed them to happen.

I created the space for these things to take place in my life. I allowed my mind to be open to thoughts, inspiration and revelations about my personal life. It was not an easy task. I walked away from the life I had. I left a job that I loved. A job I was really good at. I let go of a home that I had created a beautiful life in. I let go of my hard-earned accomplishments to allow myself to be still. To allow myself to be vulnerable to the power of the universe, to the power of my higher power and to the power of creation.

Holding on to what people think your life should look like or what you think your life should look like is a crippling epidemic of our society. Being married by a certain age, or having a specific number of children, the fanciest car or cleanest house does not matter. What people judge about your life doesn't matter. I promise you right now they do not matter. I like fancy cars and nice clothes and a clean house but they are not definitions of who I am. My relationship status does not define me. The place I live does not increase or decrease my value. It doesn't matter where the clothes I wear come from.

The absolute truth and belief that matters in life is YOU. There is not a scale of being better if you are married, single, or divorced. Where you were born, where you live now or where you grew up is not as significant as it may seem. The relationship you have with yourself is the absolute most important relationship you will ever have. The thoughts you allow in your mind about who you are and how you look are the most empowering or the most debilitating. You choose which set of thoughts you allow to control you. Any negative self-talk will deplete your spirit and the amount of joy you have in your life. You need to be you. You need to be your highest, noblest best self and no one else. The most authentic real version of who you are will out shine, out last and overcome any demon, trial or obstacle you will face. No one on this planet or in any part of the universe can be you. You are absolutely the only one. Do it, be it, live your life well and without apology every second of every minute of every hour of EVERY SINGLE DAY of your life.

PHOTOS OF ACTUAL EVENTS

Six-year Old Annie

Me with my Charlie Boy

Keys to Confidence Program (before I started crying)

Movie With My Parents

The Gigantic White Board

Date to The Lion King

www.everysingledaycorporation.com

Made in the USA
Lexington, KY
08 July 2017